GW00771963

RESPARK

Igniting Hope and Joy
after Depression and Trauma

Graham Music

Mind-Nurturing Books

First published 2022
by Mind-Nurturing Books
90 Huddleston Road, London, N7 0EG

British Library Cataloguing-in-Publication Data
A catalogue record for this book is available from the British Library

ISBN: 978-1-7398147-0-0 (pbk)
ISBN: 978-1-7398147-1-7 (ebk)
ISBN: 978-1-7398147-2-4 (large print)
ISBN; 978-1-7398147-3-1 (hbk)

CONTENTS

ACKNOWLEDGEMENTS

I would like to offer special thanks to Roger Horrocks for long ago resparking me when I was very down and flat.

A huge shout out to those who have advised me and/or read some or all of my text, including Sue Beecraft, Ricky Emanuel, Tafi Gashi, Paul Gilbert, Robert Glanz, Hayley Graham, Patrick Heaney, Josa Keyes, Shivani Lamba, Doron Levene, Sharon Lewis, Roger Linden, Mike Miller, Jane O'Rourke, Sally O'Rourke, Rachel Pardoe, Daniela Sieff, Laura Tenant, Catherine Thomas, Karen Treisman, Jo Violet, Francesca Wickers, Helen Wright.

Thanks too to Eric and Klara King for such thoughtful copyediting, and Sadie Butterworth-Jones for the cover design.

I am very grateful to all the patients who have helped me understand the issues this book describes. All clinical descriptions are either written with permission from clients or are disguised so that no one is recognisable; generally, all are amalgamations of cases.

ABOUT THE AUTHOR

Graham Music is a consultant child and adolescent psychotherapist at the Tavistock Centre and an adult psychotherapist in private practice. Formerly Associate Clinical Director of the Tavistock Clinic's Child and Family Department, his passion and clinical experience has been in working with trauma, for the last few decades at the Portman Clinic and in the Tavistock's Fostering and Adoption and Kinship Care team.

He has developed and managed a range of services working with the aftermath of child maltreatment and neglect and has prioritized community-based services for people who are often marginalized from mainstream clinic work, including developing services in over 40 schools.

He supervises and teaches in a range of trainings in the UK and abroad, delivers many keynote conference talks, and has for a long time taught internationally – for example, recently in Sicily, Istanbul, Iceland, Finland, South Africa, and Australia.

He has a particular interest in linking cutting-edge developmental findings with therapeutic practice. His publications include *Nurturing Children: From Trauma to Hope* (2019), *Nurturing Natures* (2016, 2010), *Affect and Emotion* (2001), *The Good Life* (2014), and *From Trauma to Harming Others* (co-edited with Ariel Nathanson and Janine Sternberg, 2021).

The Chief Executive of the Anna Freud Centre, Professor Peter Fonagy, wrote about his last book, Nurturing Children, that Graham Music is 'certainly one of the best and probably the most deep-thinking child psychotherapists in the world. . . . For those who wish to understand clinical phenomena and through this improve their clinical work, this book is a must.'

* * *

You can sign up for Graham Music's newsletter and other information, including blogs, publications, and forthcoming events, at https://nurturingnatures.co.uk/sign-up/ or visit his website, nurturingnatures.co.uk, and he can be contacted by:

Email: music@nurturingnatures.co.uk
Twitter: @grahammusic1
Linkedin: www.linkedin.com/in/graham-music-nurturing-natures

PART I
The spark

CHAPTER 1
WHY SPARK MATTERS, AND
WHAT IS DESPARKING?

Spark and energy

We know when we feel zest, spark, or desire, when we feel aliveness and have energy, when we feel raring to go. We also know when we lack spark, when we feel listless, low, lethargic, or flat. It generally is not a good feeling. I started writing this book during the Covid pandemic, when people were stuck inside, often isolated, some working alone, some with livelihoods at risk, others out of their depth doing home-schooling, many losing motivation. Anxiety and depression soared, and referrals to people like me increased greatly. People have felt flat, down, hopeless, and wanting a way out, to see a light at the end of the tunnel. In effect, they have lacked spark and zest.

Zest was recently found to be the character trait that most predicted resilience.[1] As defined by psychologists, it is a component of courage and is associated with being energetic, enthusiastic, hopeful, and being prepared to face challenges rather than shirk them. Zest and spark are contagious, and we like being around them, but their opposites – being listless and unsparked – are also contagious, as are many emotional states.

The metaphor of sparking is based on energy and electricity, which are central to all life. Spark can be in an individual, such

3

as when we feel fired up, and also between people, as in sparks of desire, of mutual liking, an interpersonal electricity that is almost palpable. Some of us have more energy than others, some of us feel we have too much and cannot calm down; others have too little. Personally, I veer between the two.

I have been thinking about what I call desparked states for all of my 35 years as a psychotherapist, in work with clients, teaching generations of therapists, and learning from my mentors, from new science, and of course from my own life experiences. When someone is damped down, lacks zest and spark, they can be a challenge to work with and be with. Yet such states worryingly remain insufficiently understood.

Emotional spark is an electrical metaphor. All life depends on electricity: not the man-made kind from power stations, but the kind we all need to survive. Life may possibly have grown out of sparks; some argue that meteorites, volcanos, and lightning were crucial in evolution; and, of course, we are all basically stardust. Neurons in our brains signal via electrochemical messages. Indeed, without such electrical signals in your brain and eyes, you would not be reading this sentence. Our every cell and action, every heartbeat, each muscular contraction, every thought, every communication between cells, the actions of any organ, all require electricity.

And that is a lot of energy. Herman Pontzer, in his book on metabolism,[2] suggests that each ounce of living tissue burns 10,000 times more energy than an ounce of the sun! This is harvested primarily from food and sunlight: in the case of food, by what predictably is called the 'electron transport chain'. It is no coincidence that the monster in Mary Shelley's *Frankenstein* was 'sparked' into life by electricity.

We can contrast emotional spark and energy with lifelessness, numbness, or being damped down. It is energy that differentiates being alive from being inert or dead; only living beings capture and use energy to self-replicate and act on the world. Probably like many readers, I remember seeing a creature alive one moment, then seconds later become just an inert dead body, and I tried unsuccessfully to take in what it means for life to end.

There are, though, multiple gradations of aliveness, or energetic spark. Sometimes it pays to be sparkier, like when running from an attacker, and at others to slow right down, such as when resting after working all night on a deadline. Personally, I often want to be calmer and more relaxed, but few of us want to be inanimate, or energy-less.

When we feel flat, damped down, inhibited, depressed, numbed, weak, we literally have less energy. This shows in our metabolisms. In illness, perhaps after a virus, we often feel weak. The animal who senses there is not enough food around will conserve energy by slowing its metabolism, such as by lowering heart rate and temperature, which is what we see in hibernating species, in some illnesses, and also after trauma.

Our bodies seek homeostasis – for example, by maintaining a consistent temperature, whatever the weather outside, or by giving thirst signals when rehydration is needed. A reason diets tend not to work is that our body keeps a core metabolic rate, so if we eat less, our body responds by using less calories, as bodies have set points they fight to keep. Just like our bodies, our personalities have set points, and we do not like to be pushed out of our comfort zones. If it has always felt safest to be wary or a bit rigid, it is hard to dare to shift that pattern.

Sometimes we need to find the energy to push against our usual homeostatic set points, something called allostasis, whether this is good stress or bad stress, such as the stress of fleeing danger or of growing muscle by exercising in the gym, or daring to change behavioural and emotional patterns. Then there is stasis, which implies a lack of change, being static, even stagnant, as seen, for example, in low blood flow or energy. A stagnant pool has no flow and little life in it. Stasis, stagnation, and slowing down can be a useful state to go into – for, say, a hibernating animal or a starving human – but stasis is not a place many of us want to get stuck in.

I coined the metaphor of desparking to make sense of a particular kind of stasis – that seen in de-energised and less lively states. There are times when any of us needs to conserve energy, to set aside passion, fire, zest, excitement, hope, or spark in the interests of survival. These can be appropriate responses when afflicted by stress, trauma, hopelessness, or depression. It makes sense to be flat, depressed, and shocked if we unexpectedly face a terrible loss. Healthy people and organisms recover and reboot back to normal life relatively quickly after those states. However, we can also become stuck in such energy-less states long after it is productive. I aim to provide a roadmap for resparking from such lifeless states.

Contracting and quietening for safety:
personal stories and science

As a kid I had many embarrassing and unsavoury habits, which were mainly in the service of closing down my feelings. One was sucking on my school tie, so that it developed a nasty texture and an unrecognisable shape. Others included constantly twisting my hair around my fingers (yes, pre-baldness, still with beautiful curly locks!), another was jiggling my legs when others hoped I would sit still, and yet another included a song going around in my head obsessively, which was especially helpful for ignoring pain when trying to win cross-country races (it often worked). I was also highly, or hyper-, sensitive, flinching at loud sounds, and anticipating danger around every corner. For me, powerful feelings were difficult to manage, and I needed to defend against them. Once I hit adolescence, I escaped from hormone-induced overwhelm by reading a book a day – the more complex and philosophical, the better. While this opened my mind and vistas, it also stopped me from feeling feelings that I could not manage.

Many of my quirks arose from trying to manage being sent away to school as a nervous 9-year-old. My defences were examples of contracting in the face of anxiety, of attempts to push away feelings that were too much to bear. Such defences give rise to a tightening in our muscles and in our very being, a wariness of others, a lack of trust, and a closing down of hope. When in adolescence I buried my head in books, I was defending against overwhelming feelings, but also developing a contracted attitude to life. This is common. My defending helped me get by, but in the process I lost spark, hope, ease, energy. In what follows, we will explore the advantages, but also the very real costs, of such defences, and how we can reset, reboot, and respark in response.

Danger signals

When the Covid pandemic struck, people became fearful, risk-averse, and even antisocial. These are appropriate responses to danger. However, after threat or trauma it can be hard to know when it is safe to come out of our shells. Fear and anxiety are not easy to shake off, and they can become states we get stuck in.

When danger looms, we tend to go quiet and still. Most mammals go numb and 'play dead' when faced with a predator. Even bacteria become inert when under threat – for example, going dormant in the face of antibiotics, and 'rebooting' and coming alive again when the danger has passed. Our mitochondria, tiny organelles with their own DNA and present in every living being, are our primary source of energy. However, in the face of a threat, perhaps a toxin, bacteria, or virus,[3] our mitochondria immediately stop energy production and send out danger signals to other cells.

If danger is sensed, cells will stop signalling and quieten. Most animals flee or, occasionally, fight. If these strategies fail, a fairly universal survival mechanism is to quieten, become still, even numb. Similar metabolic slowing and quietening processes are seen in response to psychological and physiological stressors, leading to a lowering of energy production and less communication between cells. The trick is to know when danger has passed, when it is safe to reboot, come alive, and spark again.

I describe in these chapters both more extreme unsparked states seen in clients I have worked with over the years, as well as milder desparking coping mechanisms that most of us at times resort to, and which we can come in and out of with less ill effect.

Desparking starts young. Tiny babies, when overwhelmed, perhaps left alone for too long, will try to manage by, for example, staring at a light bulb, self-stroking, or clenching muscles.[4] These strategies provide temporary respite from overwhelming experiences and can be let go of when things feel better, such as when a mother returns for a cuddle. This is not true in more extreme cases, such as very neglected orphans who might have never known a loving trust or safeness to return to after shutting down, so cannot let go of defences. The same is true of children who shut down in the face of serious trauma, which can lead to such coping strategies becoming entrenched, with no belief that change is possible.

Hopelessness is not just in our minds; our bodies can take on a slumped, hunched look, can become wooden and lose spark. As the neuroscientist Antonio Damasio suggested,[5] emotions are in fact bodily states, but when we feel overwhelmed, we can also lose the capacity to be aware of when our body is signalling threatening emotions. I, for example, had no idea my tie sucking or jumpy legs had anything to do with avoiding emotions I did not even know I had.

Early origins

Infants who are emotionally secure by about 8 months of age already assume that their trusted adults, their attachment figures, will come to soothe them when they are distressed, that fundamentally the world is safe and, indeed, pleasurable. In experiments, when a parent unexpectedly leaves such an infant in a strange room, more secure infants cry or protest, signalling that they expect help, that such scary abandonment is not meant to happen. If we test their heart rate or galvanic skin response (sweating), we generally see that their bodily alarm signals have gone sky high, only to quickly return to normal when the parent returns and the infant feels relief and safeness again.

Less fortunate are infants who have parents who cannot bear

strong negative emotions, such as distress, upset, or anger. Such parents ignore their own negative feelings and also shy away from such feelings in their children. Their infants soon learn to stop showing such emotions, because expressing them risks losing their parent's approval. When their parent leaves the same strange room, the infants appear not to care and carry on as if not bothered. However, when we do the same physiological tests, such as looking at their heart rates and galvanic skin response, amazingly these infants show the same distress signals as the more secure babies.[6] So, what has gone on here? While their bodies are signalling distress, they cannot afford to express their upset or, more importantly, even to recognise the distress their own body is signalling. These infants, who seem 'no trouble' or even 'happy', in fact have closed down, desparked, and lost awareness of their distress signals.

Here we see a compartmentalising of experience, a form of dissociation. The gain is avoiding rejection by a parent, but the loss is that of not learning how to recognise one's bodily signals, such as of distress, fear, or upset, nor that such body states signify emotions that could be understood and managed. This is a form of cutting off of connection, of stopping signalling. Electrical circuits only work if the connections are working well. Connection – whether between molecules, between bodily systems, or between people – is central to energy and spark. When danger looms, we see the opposite: a shutting down against threat, a stopping of signalling, often a numbing, freezing, and disconnection from others and also from ourselves.

Should we worry more about desparking?

Feeling desparked and shut down rarely comes with living an easeful, fulfilled, and joyous life. A lot of attention is paid to people with angry, aggressive, fiery personalities, kids who fight and misbehave, adults with violent, volatile personalities, people who are 'in our faces' and nigh-on impossible to ignore. Yet the quieter, energy-less ones attract far less interest, even though they have poorer prognoses and in fact need more attention.

A lot of us can feel over-sparked these days, struggling to calm down or find stillness, being easily triggered and aroused. In such states, many of us are drawn to help, such as mindfulness; and we long for more quietness and ease. This is not the case with those in desparked states, who are already quiet, often over-regulated, and need the opposite: a way to spark, enliven, and loosen up. Those in such states have lost their mojo, energy, life-force, passion – and some, sadly, have never had it to lose.

Along an alive–to–not-alive continuum, desparked states are less alive. Hibernating animals become quiescent to see out winter, traumatised ones to see out a threat of a predator, just as do bacteria and our mitochondria. Yet we don't really want to 'see out' life: we want to live full ones, with spark, zest, and energy.

I have personal reasons for my fascination with such states of mind, as I was often in them when young and yearned for someone to reach out to me. Spending too long on computer screens or obsessing about things is one of my many ways of coping with overwhelm and not daring to live fully. It has been a big challenge to find more compassion for such states in myself and others and understand why those states developed and how to help.

Such symptoms develop initially as coping strategies, as ways of getting us through difficult moments. While we need to honour the purpose they originally served, people can get 'stuck' in such states, and we need to learn how to reset and reboot them to regain health. This includes challenging the propaganda of defensive states, voices that tell us that there is no point in risking hope, reaching out for connection, daring to change. We must proceed with caution, but also courage, if genuine transformations are to occur.

The chapters: unsparked, desparked, and mis-sparked

The chapters that follow encapsulate my attempts over decades to figure out how and why people become damped down and what the best ways are to galvanise spark. In chapter 2, I outline some of the key metaphors and the concepts I use to make sense of these states. Central to this is a model, a sequence. First, we have to ensure people feel safe, mainly through developing interpersonal trusting connections. This provides a replenishing reset, and the capacity to then reboot into more enlivened energetic states of being. The next three parts of the book demonstrate the steps to achieve this, each outlining a specific form of damping down and examining what helps and why, illustrated with both extreme examples, such as of trauma and neglect, as well as the more ordinary states any of us can get into.

In chapter 3, the opening chapter of part II, I look at what I call 'desparked' states and describe how traumatic and fear-inducing experiences can knock the spark out of people who once had some. I show how trauma can lead to people looking inexpressive, lacking energy or charge, sometimes with deadened eyes and a chronic lack of emotional ease and aliveness. I examine how to help people recover from these states, initially by ensuring sufficient safeness for danger signals to turn off, as people come to live safely in their bodies. After such 'safening', it is possible to respark. In chapter 4, I describe what is called 'learned helplessness', rather like depression, where there is little hope that things will go well. We can all feel like this sometimes, but it is far worse when frightening experiences occur very early and are ongoing, resulting in a given-up-ness, often with hangdog expressions, averted gaze, or slumped body postures. The chapter shows how recovery from hopelessness to healthy energy and potency is possible. In chapter 5, I go through a case study of someone who made a really hopeful recovery from trauma, outlining the steps needed and illustrating how it is possible to move from trauma to sparking.

Part III focuses on something different, on what I call unsparked states – in other words, people who, sadly, have never had experiences that induce healthy sparkiness. I start in chapter 6 by looking at severe neglect. Such cases, while hard to contemplate, highlight the life-limiting effect of lacking good, loving early experiences. Such neglect can mean never being sparked into life by loving attention, leaving sufferers rather wooden, lifeless, with little interest in emotional worlds, their own or those of others. The most classic examples were those unfortunate children reared in very depriving orphanages, and I describe one such child's journey back to life. In Chapter 7, I tell another story of recovery, of someone who suffered both neglectful and traumatic early experiences, leading to a dramatic retreat from life. This chapter illustrates the crucial importance of human connection in regaining hope and spark.

In chapter 8, I look at features often seen in those on the autistic spectrum, and at some similarities between these and other desparked and unsparked states, again by telling a clinical tale. I illustrate typical protective manoeuvres and forms of turning away from what can otherwise feel overwhelming. Autism is now considered a spectrum, as we all have some such traits, and most of us can recognise some of the defensive ploys I describe, and which are also commonly used by those of us considered neurotypical.

In part IV, I describe what I am calling 'mis-sparking', by which I mean states we can get into where there is energy, but it is firing in unhelpful ways and is in danger of short-circuiting. In chapters 9 and 10 I look at people caught up in an increasingly common but worrying phenomenon, that of addictive states of mind, seen, for example, in obsessional use of video games or pornography. I show how such addictive traits often originate as attempts to escape from an inner deadness towards the false promise of an aliveness offered by the object of addiction. Addictions, rather than moving towards healthy sparking, are more like the misfiring of a spark plug in an engine that badly needs servicing. Chapter 10 gives an example of turning to addictions to ward off the kind of deadening many have experienced in the COVID-19 pandemic, and we see how such isolating experiences can increase the risk of addictive behaviours.

In chapter 11 we meet another form of mis-sparking and false aliveness which masks an inner deadness, one I call mind-parenting. If early on we do not have parents or others who can be safely depended on, we might instead learn to stand prematurely on our own two feet. The people described in this chapter have used their bright and agile minds to hold themselves together. Often their minds are dazzling, even brilliant, but this is a superficial sparkiness, like shiny 'bling' and superficial lustre. Although their bodies can seem energetic, inside is a deadness and flatness that they are trying to escape by addictively using their busy lively brains. In such cases of 'mis-sparking', we see attempts to escape an inner deadness that in fact needs to be faced. The stories show how, when such painful feelings are borne, life becomes richer in hope.

The final chapter draws the book's themes together. I differentiate between two very different forms of immobilisation: a worrying kind seen in trauma-induced shut-down or neglect, and a healthy form, which includes slothfulness. Sloths are creatures with a nervous system that seems enviable to more manic people like me, who find it hard to relax. I try to think about when we should worry about slothful states and when they might be something to aspire to!

Throughout the book, my primary goal is to outline how what starts as helpful coping mechanisms can become crushing of life, passion, and hope. I show how it is possible to access an internal life force and find the courage to free up the energy needed to live more fulfilled lives.

To understand and help oneself or others requires not just a set of skills but also a willingness to undergo a journey – one that we must be fit enough to undertake. We cannot run a marathon without training, and an immersive journey with unsparked states is a kind of emotional marathon, sometimes a draining one. We need to train to be emotionally present with ourselves and others, learn to read signs of subtly shifting states, and be ready to spot and facilitate indicators of potential growth and change.

This requires being prepared to become absorbed in experiences that are difficult. For some of us, the discomfort might be in opening to heart-searing pain in ourselves or others; for others, it is in bearing scary confusion; for yet others, including me, it is daring to be hopeful and positive; and for still others (again including me!), it is daring to embrace strength, aggression, and power. We all have places we are fearful of going to but which, when embraced, can enhance growth.

Putting the lessons from this book into practice depends on developing a fine-grained capacity to read and nudge nervous systems by becoming what I have called 'nervous-system whisperers'. This means becoming more body-aware, able to note in ourselves and others subtle shifts in posture, breath, muscular tension, emotional charge, and skin tone. I also believe it requires our own body-based practices. For me, these include yoga, meditation, strength training, running, as well as my biggest struggle – learning to do little and enjoy it!

Finally, as I wrote in *Nurturing Children*,[7] one of my best therapy lessons was when my first trainer, Dennis Hyde, suggested that being in emotional trouble is like being stuck in a dark ditch. We need to reach down to the sufferer in that ditch, including to the suffering part of ourselves, but neither to get stuck there so we are both trapped, nor to remain too far above, waving from an aloof place. We need to put one foot firmly in the ditch, place the other firmly on the bank, and reach out with a strong hand and a belief and message that aliveness can be experienced outside that ditch. Unsparked ditches come in many shapes and depths, and how we position ourselves in relation to our own or another person's specific ditch will be different. We have to learn how to angle our bodies, direct our eyes, pitch our voices, frame our sentences, up- or down-regulate emotional charge, all to find the best way to reach out most helpfully to such states. How we do this so that we can respark the unsparked is the subject of what follows.

CHAPTER 2
OVERARCHING IDEAS AND RECURRING METAPHORS

I have integrated ideas and metaphors – some new, some adopted from the work of others – to form a theory about what I call *desparking*, what it means to lack spark, and how we can help people come out of these states.

Sparking is the book's central metaphor. We need to *respark* to recover from numbing, lifelessness, dulling, and deadening – from *desparked* or, worse, *unsparked* (never sparked), states. We can also see *mis-sparking*, when there is much noisy, manic misfiring. Good emotional connection with another is what breeds ease, life, confidence, and zest. All sparking requires connection, whether physically, within electrical circuitry or neuronal and synaptic connections, or psychologically, between bodily energy systems. Most central are the sparks of interpersonal emotional relating. An infant's first object of desire is usually a parent, and from birth on infants are driven to connect. When this fails, such as occurs in emotional neglect or trauma, connection shuts down and spark wanes as defences are erected.

Hence the second metaphor is of **danger signalling**, which leads to erecting *defences*. When danger looms, it makes sense to mount a defence, whether turning away, fleeing, fighting, or numbing. Defences can be physical, such as bracing when confronted by an aggressor or going numb in the face of a predator. Defences can also be psychological, such as when we push away unwanted thoughts or feelings that are not deemed to be acceptable, such as a racist thought one is ashamed of.

In a castle, one might pull up the drawbridge to keep out danger, disconnecting in the interest of safety. In a similar way, feeling threatened leads to a closing down of connection to others, a wariness, a 'dis'-ease. Such quiescence and disconnecting happens even at a cellular level. When our mitochondria – sub-cells that are the energy powerhouses of our cells – sense a threat, they shut down energy production and signal danger, so that much communication within the body between cells and organs stops. This is what Robert Naviaux has called the cell danger response,[3] and it occurs when defending against threats such as toxins or parasites, and also psychological trauma.

After trauma, our brains are alert to danger, as are our nervous systems. Humans, like most organisms, learn from experience, and the learning becomes engrained in our minds, bodies, and even our cells. This leads to the next metaphor, of **priors** and **predictions**. Our previous experiences give rise to non-conscious expectations or predictions. Our brains and bodies are constantly sensing our environment, and making decisions about whether there is danger or safety, whether we should brace or relax. We all come to each moment with a lifetime of learning, of expectations, what neuroscientist Karl Friston calls *priors*,[8] which are the prisms through which we interpret the world and decide how we should respond in the current moment.

For example, I worked with a boy who had been adopted after living with his violent, frightening, and inconsistent biological parents. His priors included that no adults could be trusted and that loud noises signify danger. In fact, his priors meant he often made what we call *prediction errors*, such as wrongly predicting that his kind new adoptive father would be violent. We all make prediction errors, such as mistaking a twig for a snake or wrongly seeing a snarl on a face. Such predictions, which exist out of consciousness, can be made conscious and brought into the light, where they can lose their power. The adopted boy did not recognise his new mother's kindness as kindness, and the deep belly-laugh of his adoptive father was not seen as big-hearted. Learning to trust in kindness or big generous hearts would require a major recalibration of his belief system and of his threat-signalling nervous system.

When a threat looms, we 'clam' up, creating a barrier between ourselves and potential danger. Even plants do this – *Mimosa pudica*, for example, closing its leaves when it experiences a potentially dangerous stimulus. But biological and psychological systems can get stuck in such danger responses, not knowing the threat has passed, like an alarm bell ringing loudly long after any intruder has gone.

My next metaphors are **safening**, **resetting**, and **rebooting**. Whether in illness, such as post-viral syndromes like long Covid, or toxin or mould exposure, or psychological trauma or neglect, we can only heal once our bodies or nervous systems can trust that it is safe to lower alarm signals. In autoimmune diseases, inflammatory cytokines can continue fighting a threat that no longer exists. Similarly, after trauma, people such as that adopted boy do not believe it is safe to trust, to relax, to feel the ease, joy, and sparkiness that I so wished he felt.

When alarms signals are inappropriately firing, people need what I call **safening**: the creation of a climate of safeness that allows the turning off of danger signals. Without this, we cannot access any goodness that is out there. Even the mimosa with closed leaves cannot receive the lifegiving energy of sunlight. If I shut down emotionally in fear, as the adopted boy did after his traumas, I might survive an immediate threat, but while closed up, I cannot take in the 'sunlight' of emotional support that could help me grow and thrive.

Warm rays, such as of love, empathy, compassion, and emotional connection, facilitate safening, allowing us ultimately to say a 'yes' rather than a 'no' to experience. When we feel safe our nervous system can relax, which allows the possibility of a kind of **resetting**, almost a healing cycle, rather similar to when one is ill and needs recovery time. This can be like a healthy hibernation and hopefully is replenishing, a restoration of health and ease, which can then allow what I am calling a **rebooting**, a moving back into life with energy.

When under threat, a host of physiological processes that are active when we feel safe are turned off . To heal from trauma, dissociation, numbing, and neglect requires a receptivity to these signals sent out by our own and others' nervous systems. I call this **nervous-system whispering**, helping us to work out if we or someone is ready to be sparked or, instead, is overwhelmed and needs help to enhance safening.

When our nervous system senses safeness, our heart rate is lower, our musculature relaxed, we have healthier heart-rate variability (the space between heartbeats), we breathe more deeply, and we have more access to circuitry in the brain involved in reflection, empathy, and complex thinking, especially areas of the prefrontal cortex. When threat is present, survival trumps relaxation, our stress system fires up, and we go into survival mode, with a faster heart rate, release of adrenaline and cortisol, and tense muscles. Here, the brain circuitry involved in threat, including our amygdala, goes on high alert, and the periaqueductal grey triggers swift survival responses, including preparation for opioid-led analgesic pain relief – in other words, numbing.

Only after these danger signals turn off and we experience trust and safeness, again at a bodily level, can we heal, reboot emotionally, and spark. To move confidently into the world with zest and healthy spark, we need something inside to trigger hope. To describe this, I use the idea of an internal **lifegiver**, a concept coined by the psychoanalyst Neville Symington,[9] denoting an unconscious part of the self on the side of desire and courage, a kind of encouraging internal parental voice, enabling us to risk change and optimism.

A *lifegiver* only comes into its own once safeness is in place; it can then help us act from a sense of hope, enabling the development of what Joan Halifax[10] described as *strong backs, soft fronts, and wild hearts.* In desparked states, there is often the opposite: a floppiness, lack of backbone, a lacklustre lack of energy. If we feel someone 'has our back', we can go forward with confidence. Damped-down states are often visible in body postures and musculature, such as being hunched or contracted, while emotional health comes with being outward-facing and open to experience, not closed against possibility.

Central to resparking is healthy tension. When I am too tense or wired, I cannot take in goodness, but neither can I when I am flat and lacking energy. Rather, we want sufficient muscularity alongside the flexibility to 'roll with' experience, a solid backbone allied with an open heart – indeed, also a *wild heart.* Sparking requires some capacity for wildness!

Such healing, safening, and sparking nearly always has its roots in good emotional connection in which nervous systems are communicating with each other. Scans show that when mothers and babies are lovingly enjoying each other, their brain waves and heartbeats are in sync.[11] This is energetic electrical connection at its healthiest, a kind of synchrony we also see in people who sing together in choirs, and in good teacher–pupil or therapist–client relationships, in each case giving rise to a lowering of stress hormones and a heightening of feel-good neurotransmitters like oxytocin.

Thus, we resonate and affect each other at a bodily, cellular level. Zest, as I have suggested, is infectious, but by the same token so is dullness. One person can either respark or despark another. To become whisperers to nervous systems, we need a nuanced sensitivity to body-states, including our own, to read, for example, when someone's constricted throat means they need safening, or when their bodily tension signifies a readiness to embrace strong feelings and spark.

The 'yes', the soft front and wild heart, is also a yes that includes being open to facing scary or difficult experiences. If I am fearful of jumping into water (which I am!), I can analyse it all I like, but in the end I need to trust an internal lifegiver that helps me find the courage (*wild heart*) to face my fear, leap in, and 'take the plunge'. Such learning is in our bodies, in our cells, rather than in our heads.

My final metaphor is of a **capacious container**, derived from the work of the psychoanalyst Wilfred Bion.[12] In containment, instead of closing down against and avoiding an experience, we take it in, process, digest, and detoxify it so it loses its dangerousness. This happens when someone is with us with compassion in our dark moments. Such a container is capacious because it has space in which experiences can be metabolised and processed, leading the person to become less overwhelmed.

Emotional health comes with a roomy ability to bear a range of feeling states, to 'fold in' to our being aspects of ourselves we might otherwise disown. As an adolescent, I had to deny and hide from myself and others much that I felt, like insecurity, vulnerability, jealousy, or hurt. My relief was palpable when, in my twenties, Rachel, my first ever therapy-informed friend, helped me to understand that it is ok to have such feelings. Rachel's empathic acceptance gave rise to a more capacious version of me, one in which there was room for feelings like jealousy, enabling me to lower defensive danger responses, such as about the fear of being judged. This allowed my whole being to relax and literally to breathe more easily.

Sometimes our danger responses do not lower so easily. It makes sense that a very neglected child would not easily open to love, nor a traumatised one to overwhelming memories, nor a depressed submissive person to their potential power. To take in a new reality that challenges our priors requires what the poet T.S. Eliot described as 'daring to disturb the universe',[13] which in turn requires bravery.

This will become clear in the pages that follow, where we will meet a range of characters in shutdown states, states that all developed for understandable reasons and could only be relinquished with courage, after experiencing a sufficient sense of safeness. It would feel foolhardy for that adopted boy to suddenly trust an adult just because that adult sees themselves as kind and empathic. Defensive drawbridges and signals of danger are survival mechanisms, but they come with costs as well as gains. I describe how we can move out of such desparked states and learn to trust in the possibility of safeness, caring relationships, and the good, indeed exciting, things that life can offer.

PART II
Resparking after having lost spark

CHAPTER 3

BACK TO LIFE AFTER TRAUMA AND DISSOCIATION

Trauma

As a nervous 7-year-old in a new school, I remember the fear and terror when a tough local kid picked on me. I was threatened and tried to hide wherever I could – the toilets, the classroom, a shed, anywhere. A teacher ordered me to go out into the playground, and I knew what was coming. The bully sauntered up to me, snarling and scowling, and shouted my name, his fist raised. In that moment I felt terrified, my legs becoming jelly. I was rooted to the spot, barely breathing, my stomach knotted, knowing I had nowhere to flee. As he started to hit me, I tried to fight back. I had never fought anyone, and, sadly, this story did not have a good ending, as I was kicked and hit and, in my memory, surrounded by taunting kids. The next time it happened, there was no muscular tension: I went floppy, faint, felt sick, and wanted to urinate. Shutting down, as I did, is a classic response to danger, in our cells and metabolisms and both bodily and psychologically.

I became insular, inward, and could not tell anyone. This went on for weeks, and I remember the feeling of going cold, immobilising, and, on several occasions, almost watching myself from outside my body as I was punched. Luckily, in time the bully left the school, and I also could redeem myself, mainly as I was good at sports, which allowed me a modicum of acceptance, even popularity. However, I had regular nightmares and inside felt ashamed and terrified. Something of the numbness and bad memories remained for decades, until my own therapy brought me back to myself many years later.

My reactions, such as terror and immobilisation, are typical of trauma. In most danger responses, we see a stilling and shutting down. Trauma is, by definition, overwhelming and sometimes life-threatening, and often leads to survival responses of numbing and quietening. Other animals, and indeed even plants, bacteria, and mitochondria, do this, going still when threat is present. In humans, we also see a shutting off from painful feelings and memories.

Dissociative processes start young. The psychoanalyst and infant researcher Beatrice Beebe captured video of a mother from a trauma background who loomed with aggressive facial gestures over her 4-month-old, who in turn started to wince.[14] Yet in a microsecond this tiny infant changed the wince into a placatory smile. This baby had already learnt that feelings of distress were not tolerable to her mother, possibly due to her mother's own trauma. Already this young baby was hiding such feelings from her mother, and also herself, in effect dissociating and not even aware that she had feelings of distress or fear.

In trauma, people can literally become 'thoughtless', go into a stupor (stupefaction), and become speechless. This is understandable when faced with a life-threatening event, such as an attack by a predator. The people who suffer the most worrying symptoms have experienced not just one but multiple early traumas. If someone was consistently exposed to terrifying events, such as being tortured or witnessing or being the victim of violence or sexual abuse, they will spend a lot of time in or on the verge of such shutdown.

Trauma leaves people feeling unsafe to the core of their beings. This requires a particular kind of help. If I have been traumatised and am dissociated, attempts to liven me up, to get me to enjoy myself or be more active, could backfire. After trauma, we struggle, for example, to know or express feelings, to face memories, or to respond to playfulness. Indeed, the very idea of being livened up and starting to feel feelings can provoke anxiety and fear, especially as feeling feelings is associated with re-experiencing trauma symptoms that victims shut down in order to avoid.

Naïve therapy

For many years, despite being trained as a psychotherapist, I did not understand trauma and its effects. Consequently, I made many mistakes, employing well-intentioned if naïve approaches that were common among therapists until recently. Indeed, trauma was barely talked about or recognised before the 1970s, and only in recent decades have our understandings deepened.

Like many in the helping professions, I had personal reasons for being good at understanding other people's feelings, especially their distress. It helped in my family to be hyper-responsive to mood changes and know how to calm others. I later found that these are excellent skills for being a psychotherapist. Listening, staying with upset, hearing people's painful stories, were what I did well. In my personal therapies, I experienced relief when my own feelings were heard and I was helped to process distressing life-events, some genuinely traumatic, that I had brushed aside.

Life felt richer as I became braver about facing such difficulty. Most therapies teach that when painful feelings are heard, borne, and expressed, this can bring relief. Yet I soon learnt that sometimes this did not work, that this was often not helpful with trauma, and this left me feeling out of my depth.

New understandings of trauma explain why it can be vital to tiptoe slowly up to, or even sidestep, pain. First of all, we need to build safety-based feeling states that help turn down danger signals. Traumatised people need safeness first. Putting them in touch with their trauma too quickly can be like prodding an open wound with a sharp instrument, triggering re-traumatisation and redoubling defences such as dissociative states and flashbacks.

Trauma, by definition, is overwhelming. Flashbacks feel as though terrifying past events are happening in the present. This is why the reset, reboot, and safening stages are so important, building a personality capable of believing in ease, calm, and trust, forming a secure internal safe base-camp that is always there and from which to revisit and process difficult experiences. Hence, many newer forms of trauma therapy, such as Compassion Focused Therapy[15] or EMDR[16], expend much effort building up what they call resources: inner states that feel safe, easeful, and self-caring. These might include breathing techniques or imagining a safe place or a compassionate nurturing figure who can be turned to. These are all ways of stimulating the calming aspects of our parasympathetic nervous system. The important thing is to turn off danger signals, to learn to trust in safeness, without which pain and trauma can never be processed. In resetting, we turn off alarm signals by safening, leading to ease and trust, to opening as opposed to contracting, to softening rather than rigidity and distrust.

Flights from feeling: Mendy

This soon became clear when I first met Mendy, a late adolescent. He was referred after being the victim of a vicious gang attack, in which the friend accompanying him was brutally stabbed. Mendy was referred to an adolescent psychotherapy service for help, and I over-optimistically assumed that he was ready to talk about and process the assault and try to put it to rest.

On meeting, he seemed appropriately nervous, if somewhat edgy. When I asked if he wanted to talk about recent events, he became agitated, moving his body jerkily, sweat appearing on his brow, his eyes far away. I found myself holding my breath anxiously, my mind seemingly blanking, resonating with his shutdown in a way I have since experienced with other traumatised patients.

It is worth imagining Mendy's experience. The beating he suffered was extremely severe, made worse by his being powerless to help his friend. He remembered little of the incident, which is common after trauma. He had gone into a kind of numbed state, sometimes wrongly called the freeze response, an ancient defence mechanism used in the face of life-threat and overwhelming pain. We numb down, literally having an analgesic opioid release that stops pain, with breathing becoming shallow and heart rate lowering dramatically – a response called bradycardia. We might even feel as if we have left our body, and many sexual abuse victims describe watching their abuse from above.

This is shut-down, much like that seen in cell-danger response. Body temperature reduces, vocalisation stops, and we see tonic immobilisation, a kind of paralysis. Other symptoms include pupils dilating and sweating. Of course, looking dead enhances the chances of survival, as most predators will not risk eating something that might be toxic.

Just before such extreme responses is when we are likely to see freeze, which is a more alert state. In freeze we are preparing, sometimes bracing, and the options of either fight or flight remain open to us. In freeze we are immobile, with lowered heart rate,[17] but probably orienting, scanning the environment, non-consciously taking in signs of immediate danger, preparing to actively make ourselves safe. If this fails, we move to the next stage, from freezing to tonic immobility.

All this is relevant to Mendy. When attacked by the gang of youths, he realised he could not fight back, or even run, so he was left helpless, with only the last-resort strategies of numbing or flopping available to him. In fleeing, one retains some control; it is energising and requires activity and hope, fight responses even more so. Mendy did not have these options.

Mendy did, in fact, already have a predisposition to numbness. His father had been violent towards his mother, his siblings, and himself, and he had been a fearful, introverted child. Possibly his attackers unconsciously picked up his potential victimhood in his gait, as research has shown perpetrators can.[18] He knew in his bones about shut-down, fear, and terror but had little bodily understanding of the opposite, of what it feels like to control one's destiny, to fight, to have real power or agency.

When I had naïvely asked Mendy about what happened, he became agitated but then withdrawn, his gait robotic, showing signs of moving into what is called catalepsy, an immobility related to that seen in catatonic states. He admitted he was often assailed by flashbacks, leaving him feeling unsafe about even leaving his home.

Such numbing is a sensible adaptation, but it comes at a cost. His very slow heart rate, and acting submissive or 'dead', were helpful defence mechanisms. Even his dissociation was helpful in freeing him from overwhelming thoughts and feelings. His body and nervous system believed that threat was present, and such beliefs would not be shifted by a naïve therapist suggesting that it is helpful to talk about trauma. It has taken me years to learn to tiptoe carefully around trauma, and I still often naïvely blunder in and make things worse.

Mendy was a mixture of too floppy and too tense, with little in-between. His movement lacked grace and ease; he was constantly vigilantly expecting danger – which was understandable, given his experiences. His breathing was shallow, he felt little ease, and any energy was in the service of turning away for self-protection, closing down, not turning towards experience. Life and liveliness were terrifying, memories were traumatising, and what Mendy needed more than anything was safening, help to feel ease and turn down his cell-danger response.

Not feeling real and safening

Mendy's traumatic experiences, on top of a violent childhood, led to classic dissociative symptoms. Feeling unreal after dissociation often takes two forms, sometimes seen as one syndrome, called DPDR, meaning depersonalisation and derealisation. Depersonalisation (DP) means feeling detached from yourself, as if watching yourself from the outside, like in a movie. This is perhaps why the film *The Truman Show* struck a nerve for so many. In depersonalisation, people are out of touch with body sensations, often unable to feel emotions; they can feel robotic, and their mind can seem 'fuggy', as if wrapped in cotton wool.

Derealisation (DR) is similar, but here the external world and sometimes other people do not feel quite real. Mendy described watching events and people as if through a veil or a glass wall. Sometimes sufferers have a heightened awareness of their surroundings, with a distorted sense of how large or small, near or far, objects are. Possibly this helps in traumatic events. If someone comes at you with a knife, you will be hyperaware of that knife; it will loom very large, but other objects will not. Yet, paradoxically, things can also feel blurry and colourless. This possibly comes with the need for distancing from experiences, which takes the emotional tone and hue out.

Behind his compliant smile, Mendy was quite numbed. Teachers would get frustrated with him, and he would be targeted for being stubborn, not concentrating, and was teased for being boring. Mendy was often 'spaced out', and when with him, I could feel spacey too, not fully present. Not feeling his own bodily presence would have been protective when being beaten, by his father and by his attackers. Working with DPDR is difficult, in part because sufferers have an awareness that something is not right, and they can feel hopeless. DPDR is not something you can change just by trying harder. One cannot try to feel real!

Change is slow and incremental and follows what we might call an order of operations. Mendy needed first of all to feel safe; we needed to turn down the danger signals, which is rarely easy, as defences that develop as protection are not let go of lightly. We have to become nervous-system whisperers who help an over-alert nervous system believe that there is no longer real danger. Only then can there be a quieting, one known in one's body, not by cognitive persuasion or efforting, but deep down, almost at a cellular level.

I have learnt the importance of making the environments of sufferers as safe and untriggering as possible, whether at home, at work, or in therapy spaces. If we do not do this, any positive change gets undone. With Mendy, I started with a classic activity: orienting – in other words, checking out the space, carefully looking around the room, with me supporting him. Orienting is something we often see in an initial freeze reaction; it is a kind of response preparation, one in which heart rate tends to come down, giving some sense of control and potential for decision-making.

From here we could move on to helping him feel safer in his body. There are multiple ways this can happen; there is no rule-book, each person being different. I often start with deepening the breath. With Mendy, this did not work and only increased his panic. I used other techniques, such as trying to imagine a time and place in which he had felt safe and getting to know the accompanying feelings of safeness in his body, such as of relaxed muscles and warm feelings in his chest. He remembered a kindly female neighbour who gave him respite from his angry father. I asked him to recall what being with her had felt like, what his body remembered about the safeness she provided, what he felt when she showed kindness. This is basically building memories, forming a new embodied experience of feeling safe. He found imagining the presence of such a compassionate figure helpful and reassuring, presumably aided by the safeness he felt with me. Compassionate figures can take the form of a person once known, or a religious figure, or even a loved pet. Mendy also picked Nelson Mandela, and when he conjured him up, he felt calmer and safer. He put a picture of him up in his bedroom and could return to it for some peace.

Although Mendy became triggered if I worked with his breath, I could slowly help him be in touch with basic body sensations, such as the feeling of his feet on the floor or his buttocks on a chair. From here we could move to body-scan techniques such as the feelings in his fingers or toes, the pulsing of blood flow, an awareness of aches and pains, or the sensation of the breath moving in his chest. These are ways of grounding and learning to be more present and safe. We had to go cautiously, because for Mendy, as for many others, it understandably felt dangerous to feel physical sensations.

Once a feeling of safeness begins to be built, other changes can follow, such as deeper breathing, moments of relaxation, an increased sense of trust. Increased trust and ease, with a safe experiencing of body sensation, are prerequisites for building the capacities to process trauma. I often liken this to the experience of one's fingers thawing out after being frozen. It can tingle and hurt, we might resist it, but we know it will be for the best in the end. Unfreezing from trauma needs to be very gradual.

Slowly, Mendy made use of these interventions, and by the end he could go out into the world, to shops or places of work, and feel more confident and less fearful. Now, when realising he was triggered, he could notice that his breath was quickening and his chest tightening, and he could slowly re-regulate himself, by, for example, feeling his feet on the floor or watching other bodily sensations. His increasing ability to be aware of his body was the real turning point. Watching his pulsing sensations, his muscles tensing, noticing when he wanted to flee, enabled the slow thawing of his DPDR symptoms. He could be more present with his experiences, including memories of trauma and their accompanying body sensations. This gave him confidence to go out into the world with more hope, less fear and contraction, and increased faith that he could feel safe and, in time, be an active participant in life.

Summary

In this chapter I have described how deadness and lack of spark can be the unfortunate legacy of a need to not feel, to dissociate, in the face of overwhelmingly terrifying experiences. Numbing, instead of feeling or remembering, can help people to survive terrible experiences, but there is a cost to this. Symptoms such as dissociation and DPDR need to be treated with great respect: they cannot be bashed down or pushed through. For traumatised people, emotional sparking can feel threatening. We need to proceed with caution to help believe in a life in which feelings can be manageably felt again.

Much of the work I did with Mendy was to slowly turn down danger signals, to trust in safeness, to know that danger was not as present as his body believed. We needed to build the conditions for a genuine healthy recharging, while avoiding short-circuits, overheating, and shutdowns. After the reset, reboot, and lowering of danger signals, the potential was there for an increase in energy, a readiness to spark into life. In the next chapters we see how, after safening, spark can safely and healthily be injected so that people can embrace life more fully.

CHAPTER 4
RIPE FOR SPARKING

Sparking aliveness after depression and learned helplessness

Energy – or the lack of it – is the central motif of this book. Many people lack spark, energy, life-force, or what Freud called *libido*. For some, that spark never developed (unsparked), while for others it was repressed or deactivated (desparked) and needed freeing or loosening up.

Desparking can happen in a small way, such as when feelings are repressed because they are deemed unacceptable. For example, in my family, it was not all right to show feelings of jealousy, anger, or competitiveness. Repressing feelings can dam up energy, as opposed to letting it flow. As we have seen, this can start at a young age. Babies whose parents cannot bear their distress learn to inhibit expressions of their own distress and to not even know they feel it. At the root of this is a form of fear, such as of losing a parent's approval or love, which children cannot afford to do.

Parental and societal expectations, what Freud called the *superego*, are mechanisms for repressing desires, thoughts, and feelings that are unacceptable to people we depend on. This can leave people experiencing conflict between an urge, such as an illicit sexual wish, and the need to disown it, and such conflicts are in themselves anxiety-producing and desparking.

For example, I remember being in a therapy group some 30 years ago when a woman who later became a valued colleague complained about builders wolf-whistling her in a way she experienced as sexually intimidating. I felt for her – I still do, for women accosted like that. I also immediately felt guilty. In fact, I even felt bad that I was a man with sexual desires, the expression of which could cause another person pain. I and two other men sat still, silent, shamefaced, while other women supported my colleague. Then a fourth man in the group baulked at the tone of the discussion, stating baldly that, while he did not want to upset anyone, he wanted to feel ok about having sexual desires and not to feel ashamed of this. Some of the women said how helpful it was to hear this and described a bind they experienced: they liked being appreciated and did not want not to be noticed, but equally did not want to feel intimidated. I felt huge relief, but also a bit silly, and realised how often shame and guilt got in the way of allowing myself to feel ok about what I was really feeling.

Shame has physical correlates, such as blushing or a hangdog expression. If I am fearful of being told off, or, worse, beaten or attacked, the likelihood is that I will act in a submissive way. Evolutionary theory describes a social ranking system, in which lower-ranking animals defer to those of higher status, their submissiveness taking a physical as well as a psychological form. In animals, this might be lying on one's back, exposing one's belly, and in humans it might be making oneself smaller, such as by slumping or taking a lower seat.

A more extreme example of fear is seen in what Martin Seligman called learned helplessness.[19] In rather cruel experiments, in which dogs were given electric shocks, some dogs could stop these by pressing a lever, while others had no such opportunity. The dogs with no control did not try to escape, even when it was possible to do so. In effect, their 'learned helplessness' became a kind of character trait, the animals becoming fearful and hopeless and showing symptoms very like human depression and anxiety. Many people I have worked with could be described as having had their spirits broken by both fear and a lack of control over their fate.

The psychiatrist Viktor Frankl, himself an Auschwitz inmate, reported that many concentration camp survivors, when liberated, initially walked out of the gates but then returned, to lie down within the camp borders. They could not believe that freedom was really in their grasp. This is what we see in many traumatised people who do not protest against violence or abuse and take on a given-up, hopeless stance. This includes children or adults who have been victims of sexual, domestic, or racial violence and are too accepting of their lot.

We all repress and deny many thoughts and feelings out of anxiety, fear, or guilt, but such repression has an effect, often leaving us feeling less alive. Learned helplessness, though, is a much more worrying quashing of life, a trauma-induced fear resulting in a paralysis that remains well after the perpetrator has gone. This is often seen in people's bodies, such as slumped poses, heads bowed, fearing to stand tall.

I know this only too well in myself, having often felt paralysed by fear, expecting judgement and criticism and, when things go wrong, blaming myself. Like many children who had parents who could easily anger, I often felt cowed, fearful, and would give up and withdraw. I remember one teacher noticing my forlorn look and saying how sad my eyes were, for which I still feel grateful. I did not know I had sad eyes. I certainly was too fearful and self-blaming to be angry. Most children, of course, cannot afford to get cross with their parents, and so blame tends to be directed inwards, back at themselves, which was what I did, and what I have seen in countless kids from abusive backgrounds. This was beautifully described long ago by the psychoanalyst Ronald Fairbairn as the moral defence,[20] in which it feels safer to be bad in a world ruled by a good God, than to be good in a world ruled by the devil.

Psychotherapists work hard to help people manage painful feelings, to mourn, grieve, allow vulnerability, which are all immensely important. However, for the kinds of states I describe here, something more active and energising is needed. Rage and anger are appropriate responses to abuse and trauma and should not be bypassed.

If a colleague attacks me, or my partner slaps me, it can be healthy to fight back, to feel strength instead of retreating into helplessness and given-upness. However, anger can be scary: we might fear being hit again or alienating someone we need. When asked how they feel about what happened to them, many victims say things like, 'perhaps I deserved to be hit', or 'I should not have done that', or 'but I know he loves me, really'. These rationalisations keep people from feeling what is below the surface, such as upset, hurt, and, possibly more importantly, anger.

Rationalisation occurs when we move away from feelings into thoughts, a movement that often happens because feelings such as rage are unnerving. Learned helplessness often leads to such defensive manoeuvres. What is needed, instead, is help getting closer to righteous anger, rage, and protest, really knowing and owning such feelings, in one's body, and in the depths of one's being. This enables people to become less fearful and more confident that they can become powerful, strong, and energised.

From fear to courage: Khenan

Hopefully, these ideas will become clear on meeting Khenan, a mixed-race young man from a complex background. He had been subjected to racial abuse and also bullied at school, and at home was attacked, both verbally and physically, by his stepfather, the father of his two younger half-siblings. He was a sad young man when I met him, nervous, unconfident, and awkward, getting through life with a false grin and staying under the parapet. Although not slumped like many in unsparked states, he had a lack of solidity and a poor sense of his worth.

He could not look people in the eye; he had an elusive quality, always seeming about to retreat, as if other people were not to be trusted. He carried deep pain and sadness just beneath the surface, and, further hidden, was rage. At home he could spend hours staring into space or at computer games. He complained of many physiological symptoms of the kind we often see in our smooth-muscle system when there is unprocessed, denied emotion. Smooth-muscle presentations include symptoms such as, for example, irritable bowel syndrome (IBS), migraines, nausea, diarrhoea, the need to suddenly urinate, or back pain. Physiologically, smooth muscles are in the digestive tract and blood vessels, out of conscious control. When we learn to feel unprocessed denied feelings, such as rage and anger, it is surprising how often such smooth-muscle-led symptoms disappear.

Things often become more complex when race enters the picture, possibly even more so for young black men. Khenan wanted to be cool, as well as strong and tough – aspirations of his peer group. He was liked by teachers, but his academic potential was never taken seriously. Perhaps typically of black youth, he was encouraged in sports, and when he demonstrated a quicksilver ability on the football field, the bullying stopped, and he could stay even more under the radar, with his big smile, gliding around the dangers of group life, friendships, and adolescence, rather like he glided past tackles on the football pitch. I personally empathised, as being good at football and sports had saved me from an awful adolescence and brought me some sense of self-worth.

Yet, in truth, Khenan was very unhappy, often on the edge of imploding, or exploding, barely managing the powerful feelings that were taking him over. His overt reason for coming to therapy at the age of 16 years was a painful experience of an unrequited crush on an older boy, leading to desperate near-suicidal feelings. Khenan had reluctantly admitted to himself that he was gay, not something he embraced, and, given the homophobic adolescent culture he inhabited, this increased his sense of inadequacy.

Initially when we met, he seemed too ashamed to look at me. I could barely make out his face beneath his hoodie and scarves. He looked awkward, distant, seeming almost not to be in the room with me. He was worried about being judged, especially about his sexuality, and could barely string a sentence together. Such incoherence is typical of the cognitive dissonance often seen in emotional overload. This links with what happens in trauma, where Broca's region in the brain, needed for speech, can go offline. As with Mendy, the initial work was about developing a sense of safeness, helping him feel at ease in his body, and trying to find some self-compassion instead of shame and self-hatred, about himself and his sexuality. First, emotional connection, trust, and a shared language needed to be built between us, and this took many months. After all, why would he trust me, an older male from a different culture?

As he relaxed, colour came to his face, his breathing deepened, and he moved with more purpose. I began to see hopeful signs of healthy striated muscle tension, the kind that suggests someone is ready to face feelings. In his case, he clenched his hands and sighed deeply, both often a sign of readiness. A look of disgust came onto his face when he described an interaction with a classmate, and I asked him to exaggerate the gesture and expand on it. For the first time I saw anger and some incipient power, a young man with strong feelings, in the room, his disgust moving into rage. There was still a lot of fudging, intellectualising, and shifting directions, and I often felt like a spear-hunting fisherman trying to pin down my prey. It is hard to get the balance between going in too hard, which can lead to smooth-muscle and dissociative defences, and going too softly and cautiously, which can mean that feelings that are ready to be faced are avoided, leaving old symptoms in place.

Resparking cannot happen when people are in withdrawn smooth-muscle states and dissociated, so a sense of safeness is vital to allow a replenishing reset. But real vitality requires energy and power, and pushing down feelings like rage or grief damps our vitalising potential. When the time is right, it is crucial that such defences are challenged, unleashing potency, hope, and a resparking of emotions. This is where we need to read another's nervous system and whisper to it and have the courage to push through defences when the time is right.

In Khenan's case, his defences made sense, as he had been bullied, abused, and demeaned; he had also, in effect, lost his mother when his stepfather came on the scene. He felt unlovable and had lost trust in adults. Like most children, he blamed himself, feeling it was he who was at fault, not the adults. He also knew, to his cost, how dangerous it could be to challenge or confront adults who were abusive, such as his stepfather. Keeping a low profile, staying below the parapet, had served him well, but at a cost.

Challenging defences

In one meeting Khenan was talking about his stepfather, and his breath quickened and his legs started to move. These were examples of striated muscle tone, which gave me the courage to ask him what the feeling was towards his stepfather: was it anger? He said yes. I asked if he could exaggerate the gesture and what he wanted to express. His immediate response was the classic 'learned helplessness' one – that he would rather not, that it's best not make a fuss. Khenan found it hard to believe that I could allow and hear his anger and help him express it. Initially he would fudge his feelings, perhaps saying that what happened was 'unfair', but when pushed, he could get nearer to real feelings like anger, even fury.

As we often see, he became more assertive, developing spark alongside his newfound confidence and becoming hopeful about possible change. He began to stand up for himself in the playground, 'holding his ground', not taking things 'lying down'. He felt more solid, with less need to glide around elusively. Such a shift can have complicated repercussions for black youth. An action viewed as courageously assertive in a white middle-class boy can be (mis)construed as threatening or dangerous in a young black man of the same age. It took courage from him, and support from me, to keep growing in this way. However, his relief was palpable; he had a life now and could sense a future. He even was no longer cowed by his stepfather, helped by now being taller than him now and having started serious strength training and learning boxing!

In cases like this, bravery is required, in all parties. Khenan needed to be challenged about his defensive manoeuvres, such as his compliant smile and evasive body gestures. We were pushing through his set-points, pushing for allostasis. It was hard for him to expand his chest, to stand up and be counted, express the rage and upset bottled up inside him. Yet that is what frees up energy, gives rise to sparking, making one feel alive. In Khenan we saw an opening up, not closing down, to life, a new litheness and muscularity, and, once danger signals had given way to safeness, he developed a greater capacity to feel feelings he had previously pushed down.

His priors were being challenged, such as that things will always work out badly for him, that he would always lose in a fight, that no one would like him, let alone find him attractive. With such changes, with feeling feelings he had previously not been able to know and own, we saw his psychosomatic symptoms, like nausea, tics, and back problems, recede considerably. This is surprisingly common. Such developments will be seen more clearly in the next chapter, where I describe the journey I went on with Laila, from shutting-down after trauma to safening and resetting and then rebooting to confidence and power.

CHAPTER 5

A JOURNEY FROM FROZEN TRAUMA TO SAFENESS AND THEN GENUINE SPARK

Immobilisation for safety: Laila

This chapter tells the story of Laila and her recovery from trauma. Laila came to see me in her mid-thirties, when she felt unhappy and desperate. She had had a tough early life, shunted between foster homes, never consistently cared for or held in mind, moving from town to town and school to school, experiencing a childhood of neglect and bullying.

She clearly needed help but, not surprisingly, was distrustful of me, as she was of most people. She had never been in a relationship, had very few friends, and lived an isolated life, although she had a series of best friends whom she stuck to like glue until, inevitably, she fell out with them, to be replaced by another. I was struck by the floppiness in her body, which could be mistaken for calmness. Therapy was a challenge, as her personality had developed around avoiding being seen, not revealing herself, staying under the radar.

As a child, Laila had been exposed to inappropriate males and might have been sexually abused, but she had no memory of this. This could have been when she first went into extreme 'flop' immobile postures, although this might have resulted from other traumatic or neglectful experiences. At school she would hide in a corner of the playground, clinging to a book, hair over her face and hoodie over her head, for fear of the next bullying episode. This is a classic response to trauma. Like all mammals, when serious danger is present, humans will become still, 'playing possum', as this aids chances of survival.

As the controversial psychiatrist R.D. Laing wrote: 'In a world full of danger, to be a potentially see-able object is to be constantly exposed to danger. . . . The obvious defence against such a danger is to make oneself invisible. . . .'[21] Of course, being visible exposes one to potential attacks, and the school playground was a danger zone for Laila.

Decades after the serious trauma, she was still living in a nightmare world of fear and constant danger signals. One could mistake her stillness for being relaxed, an all-too-common error. When people do not obviously act stressed, they can be misperceived as 'calm', even 'cool'. There is some truth in this, as after trauma, body temperature often reduces. The point of shutdown is not just to be unseen, but also to not feel what is too difficult to feel. She was barely conscious of her bodily stillness, or of the shallowness of her breath or inexpressiveness of her face. These danger responses had once served her well but now kept her from living an emotionally rich life. Laila badly needed a safening reset.

Resparking from such states is a slow process; it is all too easy to set off alarm signals again, hence the need to proceed with caution. Laila initially needed nervous-system whispering to help her feel safer in her body, to notice and make sense of fear-related bodily responses, like sweating, tensing, going cold, flinching with fear.

One of the first things I focused on was her breathing. Rather than suggesting she breathe more deeply, I first asked what her breath felt like. 'I can't really feel it', she replied. I asked her to put her hand on her chest and feel any movement. I then asked if it felt safe to loosen or deepen her breath a tiny bit and what that felt like. She did this and said it felt scary, it made her nervous. Breathing in a deep and relaxed way requires some trust that the world is safe, that there is no immediate danger. I suggested instead that she really breathe in, as if very tense, and tighten up her breath, as if in danger: 'Let's get to know what it feels like to breathe as if scared, to really hold your breath.' She did this and then said: 'I realise how constricted I am feeling, I had never noticed.' The first tears I had seen seeped into her eyes.

This was a slow, incremental process, trying out a deeper breath, seeing how it felt, then ensuring she felt safe enough to return to her comfort zone. As I often find, memories, thoughts, and feelings flooded into sessions, and we had to go carefully. Trusting in safeness often feels risky when our bodies have habitually been signalling ever-present danger.

Some weeks later I asked her to widen her shoulders, allow a breath into her belly, and let her chest (heart) open. Tears streamed down her face. She had remembered some good feelings, times with a foster carer who had loved and protected her. The image of this kind woman became a symbol of self-compassion, an inner voice she could turn to for support, who could help her trust in this new safening. She had that bitter-sweet feeling of knowing that opening up to hope would probably feel good, but still wanting to fight it, feeling the urge to shut down again, back to what she knew so well. Like all of us, she needed to know that she could return to her defences if and when she needed them.

We began to explore what it felt like to be seen and noticed, by a colleague at work, by me – the mixed feelings this evoked. She came to sessions with stories of what she was now noticing, such as how quickly she closed up like a clam when someone looked at her, or how she contracted tightly when she had an anxious thought. Becoming her own nervous-system whisperer meant she could notice herself tense up, which opened the possibility of letting such tension go. This is something that mindfulness also teaches us, allowing and making space for experiences such as tension and watching them from a more capacious containing place, almost cradling the tension rather than acting on the temptation to push it away or defend against it.

Much of the initial work with Laila was in such resetting, in safening, helping danger signals lessen, and trusting in a new sense of ease. Could she look around and feel safe and not tense up? Could she look someone in the eye and not be scared? Could she catch herself tensing and help herself by, for example, watching her breath? The first stage of resparking for Laila was with her body and nervous system, allowing a pulsing in her being, in the breath, in the sensations in her body, an aliveness she had long needed to close down against.

Sometimes this brought up memories, such as of a girl who had bullied her. I never sought out those memories, but when they arose, we worked carefully with them. The challenge is not to re-traumatise, not to re-signal danger, but to tiptoe up to trauma, gently be with it, then move back to safety, and repeat the process time and again. Safeness sets a foundation for building the equipment to process and metabolise feelings, which can then lead to rebooting and sparking.

Laila's subdued, lacklustre floppiness started to shapeshift into more toned muscularity, to healthy tension. This included the beginnings of sexual spark – in her case, beginning to get to know her attraction to other women. Her priors, such as her beliefs that 'I must stay still otherwise it is too dangerous', or 'it is safer to withdraw', were being challenged. She was developing a new repertoire alongside her old ways. Her inertia had come from paralysing fear, but now she could slowly soften, open, and feel more trust, which in turn bred life, heat, strength, and courage, indeed spark, an energetic current that could be powerful.

Moving into power and striated muscle

Soon, if triggered, she could note this and then foster an internal sense of safeness. She had made a safe haven at home, using cushions, candles, comforting aromas, and soft fabrics. She could now soothe herself when she was anxious, with breathing techniques or soft yoga poses, or wrapping herself in cosy blankets and basking in calming music. She was becoming her own nervous-system whisperer.

With this reset and new sense of security, we could begin to look at the more difficult feelings. Her floppiness, hunched pose, and lack of energy were all signs of a depressed hopelessness, an embodied belief that danger was still constantly lurking, and that she was powerless against it. When we began to think about what had happened to her, such as the bullying, she quickly went into rationalisations such as, 'well, it's all in the past now' or, worse, 'but I feel I am just a monster'. At one point, her new boss was treating her in a way that was clearly unfair, yet she could not really see this. I asked how she felt towards her boss for what he did, and she replied, 'Well I did make a mistake, I am always getting things

51

wrong.' Digging a bit deeper, we found depths of shame and self-contempt in her body, voice, and psyche.

Slowly she began to see what she was doing to herself, and what she was not doing for herself, and her lifegiver started coming into life. I began to note when she was self-deprecating with me, and how overly forgiving she was when I got something wrong. 'Oh, but you did not mean it', she would say. She was hugely invested in being 'nice', but this was a placatory niceness. For her, others needed to be 'kept sweet' or else they might hurt her.

I suggested she try to imagine what it might feel like to be angry. She had never had the relief one can feel when one's rage is accepted and the other remains steadfast, strong but non-retaliatory. As the paediatrician Donald Winnicott taught us long ago,[22] having one's rage heard and survived without retaliation helps people to know that their feelings are not dangerous and leads to a sense of having a separate self, not always having to tiptoe around potential emotional minefields. This is energising, sparking, and it facilitates an opening up to connection, not the closing down we see when danger signals are high.

Slowly Laila began to be able to stand up for herself more. At work, she challenged her boss, becoming less likely to take criticism 'lying down'. We role-played interactions in which she began to learn what it feels like to 'stand up' for herself, to 'hold her head up high' and 'look the other in the eye', rather than be submissive. This began to translate into other areas of her life. She started not to apologise, no longer saying 'sorry to ask you', or 'I hope you don't mind', but instead beginning to feel that she had a right to ask for things. Her over-zealous worry that those around her, including me, might be upset began to abate, and instead she became more assertive. I had often felt could almost blow Laila over, as if she had given away power, but no longer!

She became more able to challenge me directly. She plucked up the courage to let me know she wanted to be called 'they', not she, and in time she could become cross with what she saw as my lack of support and understanding of her sexual identity. In the end, I saw a side of her that was assertive, even acerbic and scathing. When I could hold her rage, not retaliate but try to make sense of it, she flourished. Her newfound capacity for anger seemed healthy, outward-facing, coming from a place of belief, passion, and hope.

Her body seemed to be changing: she had energy in her limbs, colour was coming to her cheeks, her chest and heart area were opening, her head held up, and she was moving with confidence, even determination, with much less hint of apology or deference. I noted this and asked what else had changed, and I was pleasantly surprised to learn that she was no longer just doing gentle 'yin' yoga but had started more active Ashtanga classes, which contain 'warrior' poses. She had even begun to do some strength training. Some muscularity was growing, in both mind and body, and she had also begun to look more vibrant. She now quite liked being noticed on the street, especially by women she found attractive. She was enjoying an increased confidence in her lesbian sexuality, dating and daring to tentatively trust in her ability to navigate intimacy. She was enjoying the beginnings of an inner strength that communicated that she was now no pushover. I had no doubt that her lifegiver was truly online and firing her into power, zest, and hope.

This was not a straightforward process; the gains came with a cost. She had to find the courage to become assertive, to feel anger and rage, to change deep patterns and priors. When her boss had preferentially privileged a colleague over her, I asked, 'So what do you want to say to him?' 'Well, he was not being very nice.' 'Okay', I would reply, 'but that is not how you feel, so how do you feel towards him for what he did?' 'Well', she might say, 'I have got used to it now.' I pushed more: 'Hmm, again that is not saying what you feel. I notice how your jaw is clenched and your fist tensed, what would they like to do?' 'Oh, nothing', she said a bit shamefaced, as she tried to let go of the tension. I clenched my own fists and said forcefully: 'I do that when I am really angry. Sometimes expressing our anger can be helpful.'

She looked interested and breathed deeper. Her default position was to be compliant, and she had justified this with a kind of moral superiority, believing that anger is bad, that being forceful is not 'nice'. This, though, came at a huge cost. I challenged her again, and she was able, with prompting, to raise her head and say how angry she was. I asked her to express the feelings, imagining her boss in front of her. As she did this, the energy in her body changed: she was leaning forward and showed real power. Anger, when expressed, tends to energetically rise upwards through the body, perhaps like sparks, the opposite of the pushing down of desparking and depression.

Afterwards we carefully debriefed. I asked how she felt. She was breathing deeply now, looking proud and definitely energised. A bit later tears came, partly of relief, and also a genuine sadness and compassion for the Laila who had always suffered by not daring to take herself seriously.

The clenched fists and jaw, as I pointed out, were classic signs of 'striated' muscle, the kind that signals that energy and tension is ready to be felt and expressed. Sometimes when I pushed Laila too far, she would retreat into physiological states that are the opposite, into energyless 'smooth-muscle' states, such as a stomach cramp, feeling faint, or a headache. When a feeling, like rage or upset, is too much to bear, then, as we also saw with Khenan, smooth-muscle presentations, such as nausea, IBS, or giddiness, often result.

We can think of smooth-muscle defences as a way of avoiding strong feelings that cannot be owned. To use some central metaphors of the book, by developing a sufficiently capacious container to allow, feel, and express repressed feelings, we develop more energy, spark, and a capacity for connecting rather than closing down. In Laila, we saw movement towards life, not away from it, healthier muscularity, a freeing of energy, and genuine sparking. One of the most exciting things about freeing such damned-up energy is that many physiological symptoms, too often termed psychosomatic, simply fade away. If we can express our rage and anger and do not need to repress these feelings, then, research shows, physiological symptoms common in smooth-muscle states decrease.[23]

Occasionally Laila struggled with what we see in more serious cases, what is called cognitive dissonance, often with deeper fragmentation, such as amnesia, bizarre thinking, or even hallucinations. When this happens, challenging defences is the last thing needed. Instead, the task is to prioritise restabilising, as I did with Laila initially, to reduce anxiety by facilitating physiological and psychological safeness.

With Laila, we would do gentle body-based mindfulness exercises, which helped her to come out of numbed states. One absolutely needs to feel safe in one's body before resparking can happen. It is only when someone feels safe enough that striated muscle signals come online, and that is when one can challenge defences against pushed-away feelings, freeing up energy and life-force. Laila's fist-clenching and jaw-tightening were classic signs of striated muscular tension, indicating that she could now bear and express her rage. This is why we need to become nervous-system whisperers; the clues are in the body, and we need to read them and help shift the physiology as well as the psychology.

Summary

In cases of learned helplessness and some forms of depression, a lack of spark and vitality is due to a loss of hope and a dispiriting lack of belief in one's potency. We saw different variants of this in Mendy, Khenan, and Laila, who all arrived with a bleak despondency deep in their beings. Through their therapy, they came back into their bodies, became outward-facing, their lifegiver actively engaged, moving towards rather than away from life, becoming able to embrace a wider range of emotions. Their priors and core beliefs were challenged, and they developed strength and vitality. The added benefit was that most of the physiological problems they presented with, the so-called psychosomatic symptoms so often seen with smooth-muscle presentations, abated.

Anger can be feared, seen as dangerous, scary, and threatening. Yet it is a vital force. The word aggression comes from the Latin *aggressionem*, meaning to 'move towards', and in living a full life we move towards experiences rather than away from them. That is a hallmark of resilience. Resilient, secure toddlers show brain patterns with greater left prefrontal activity,[24] linked with moving towards others and towards challenges, whereas the more neurotic of us move away, in fear, anxiety, and un-confidence. The lifegiver is an inner voice or force that moves us towards experience with hope and trust.

This is not just about anger and aggression. Laila spent many hours in tears, experiencing grief about her early life, the loss of what was stolen, working through deep pain, as well as remorse for her poor relationship with her family. These 'softer' feelings, while possibly in some ways deeper, are most healthy when expressed in the right time and order. In therapy, sadness, grief, and pain can be accessed too quickly, in a kind of short-cut, a therapeutic bypass, to avoid experiencing the rage and power that often needs to be felt first. Without strength, power, and confidence, damping can continue to subdue the life-force; but with it, as we saw with Laila, real sparking can and does result.

PART III

The unsparked: people whose spark never developed

CHAPTER 6

NEGLECT: POTENTIALS NEGLECTED

Avoiding feelings

My personal history includes being sent to boarding school at the age of 9, where I, alongside others my age, had to just 'get on with it', where there was no space for moping, missing parental care, or expecting emotional understanding or support. Many of us developed tough defences, exoskeletons, which helped our survival but left our needy, vulnerable selves unseen and deeply buried.

The boys who cried at night were often teased for being weak and sissies. We needed to hide our pain and despair. The psychoanalyst Herbert Rosenfeld[25] described how needy, dependent parts of the self can be disowned and denigrated, resulting in a hatred of vulnerability, in ourselves and in others. We responded like this to the crying boys, from whom we were determined to differentiate ourselves.

Warding off feelings is a helpful strategy when they are not acceptable. If given the message, when young, that one should not show feelings like despair, grief, fear, or vulnerability, most children comply. After all, we cannot afford to alienate those we depend on. Such children often assume that they must stand on their own two feet, that seeking help is a form of weakness, or that expressing feelings is silly.

When in the company of people who are emotionally cut off, we can have feelings like boredom, frustration, or lack of interest. Such feelings are hard, even embarrassing, to admit to for therapists like me, who like to be thought of as warm, empathic, and kind. Yet humans are a resonant species, and with people in avoidant states of mind I, like many of us, can find myself feeling dulled down, my thoughts becoming wooden and my bodily feelings flat. I think such resonating gives us a hint of what it must be like to live in their skin.

Most of us abhor the possibility that we could be that dull, boring person for others, someone who is seen as a 'drag'. We probably all know people whom we do not relish spending time with, because we feel flat in their presence. We can feel this with people who feel low or down, perhaps going through a bad patch, but it is worse when with people who have never had much spark. Someone who, from a young age, has had little experience of people being interested in their minds, feelings, and inner worlds is less likely to evoke interest in others.

In many cases, when we, or our nearest and dearest, feel a bit flat, it is very possible to galvanise a respark. In minor desparking, it generally takes the steps previously described: safening, empathic containment, and rebooting. Recently a friend was upset when I did not respond to a slightly veiled plea for help. The truth is, I had not spotted the signs in his email – something I might have done had I been less preoccupied. When I next saw him, he seemed withdrawn and hard to reach. He was hurt, for which I do not blame him. I knew I had to hear his feelings, bear and manage his anger (capacious containment), know and acknowledge my part in his upset. This, thankfully, was enough for him to feel safe and for us to slowly rebuild connection. Over the next hours we could talk about the issues, and we both slowly relaxed; by the end, through sharing our plights, hopes, and worries, he and I had lightened up – so much so that we could laugh and joke, re-finding our former spark.

Of course, the trick is to stay where the other person is, to empathise with them (empathy literally means to 'feel with'), not try to cheer them up too quickly, not put a false positive gloss on a situation, to avoid what one of my ex-therapists called 'pouring sugar on shit'. That never works, but when someone feels met and heard where they are, then safening, connection, and resparking can happen. The challenge is much more complex when the issues run very deep, as was the case with Lucca, whom I now describe.

A case of neglect: Lucca

Several decades ago, I met Lucca, who was 6 years old. He had been in one of the first cohorts of children adopted from the Ceausescu-era Romanian orphanages where children experienced unthinkable neglect. Not surprisingly, by the time he was placed for adoption at the age of 3 years, deeply shutdown patterns had formed. Lucca's new parents struggled to warm to him. They had had a biological child, but the mother was unable to bear more children. They had also adopted a child, Marsha, from a UK family in which there had been some trauma. They loved their biological child to bits, and Marsha was a lively bundle of energy whom they were learning to love, and who was becoming more manageable, open, and, indeed, fun. She was demonstrative, needy, and demanding, but at least she was sparkily alive.

With Lucca, things were different. They did not warm to him; he seemed flat and expressionless, living in a self-contained, detached world. He did puzzles, played with toy cars and Plasticine endlessly, but he did not seem to need other people, including his new parents. He sought no help or comfort if he had an accident, would run out into the street without looking back to his parents, and when reunited after a separation showed no pleasure, reacting to his parents as he did to strangers.

Lucca's history, like many raised in such depriving environments as those Romanian orphanages, makes sense of how he developed his priors, his beliefs that no one could be there for him. He would have been left alone, with little human contact, isolated for most of the day. He would have had to somehow hold himself together, perhaps by self-soothing, rocking, staring blankly, but definitely numbing his feelings and sensations. His experience would have been of overwhelming isolation, leading to shutting down. He would have had little experience of helpful adults, except those occasionally providing food and clothes or washing him, probably without a loving touch. He would not have been appreciated, thought about, let alone adored, and thoughts and feelings – his own and others – would have been little understood.

It was hard for his adoptive parents, as he gave so little back, and they received few of the rewards parents normally get. He seemed mostly in his own world. Even in the early family meetings, I found him hard to concentrate on and paid more attention to his siblings and parents than to him. He easily slipped out of people's minds. Having lacked the usual early reciprocal, mutually enjoyable interactions – in fact, lacking much interaction at all – he, not surprisingly, barely noticed social cues, and he easily went under people's radar.

At nursery and school, he was a loner, showing little interest in other children. He evoked little pleasure in other people, spent hours in aimless activities, and showed minimal empathy or interest in others. He was typical of children who can sit at the back of school classes unnoticed. Such children seem 'just fine', and, sadly, they rarely ask for help or evoke worry.

Neglected children tend to turn in on themselves: they have little choice. Their eyes can take on a hollow look, their bodies lacking energy or spark, and they often manage by self-soothing strategies, such as rocking. Tragically, they learn not to hope for person-to-person sustenance, and they give up on the fertiliser that grows minds and personalities. Anne Alvarez, a child psychotherapist and autism specialist, has described many as 'undrawn'[26] rather than withdrawn, parts of them having never come fully alive. Many I have worked with have not developed a 'life-force', passion, desire, excitement, or hope. They, early on, lacked what Colwyn Trevarthen[27] called 'live company', and they need help to grow a feeling-full mind, body, and heart. Otherwise, they become less than live company – for others and, indeed, for themselves.

Flatness resonates

In therapy sessions with those who have suffered neglect, both children and adults, I must shamefully admit that sometimes my mind wanders off. My bodily responses give me the needed clues, when I am alert enough to notice these – a dullness, listlessness, lack of feeling. It is a challenge to remain psychologically alive with people who easily slip out of our minds. As research shows,[28] neglected people have less ability to understand emotional expressions. Tragically, they also experience little pleasure, including in human contact, and rarely inspire hope, affection, or enjoyment in those around them.

I often felt an onset of fatigue when the receptionist told me of Lucca's arrival. When with him, my gait was stiffer than usual, and I had less bounce in my step. With such children I can feel a whole range of things, none of which I like. I can feel incompetent, resistant, sorry for myself, fed-up, and I sometimes wonder if I am in the wrong business altogether. Time passed slowly with Lucca, and with some children every second can feel like an eternity. Possibly time passing excruciatingly slowly was what his life had felt like in the orphanage, and why he engaged in numbing rituals. Yet, with Lucca and others, I knew that to make a difference I needed to find some spark of aliveness in myself to use in our work together.

It is worth stressing that the neglected people I describe have often not suffered overt trauma, such as being beaten or sexually abused or witnessing violence. More important than bad things that happened to them is what did not happen to them – omission rather than commission, not receiving the good experiences that foster healthy emotional development. The lethargy and lack of enthusiasm I felt before meeting Lucca is very different from how I feel when with traumatised and abused children, who can be aggressive and reactive, and with whom I am generally on edge and anxious, but emotionally present. Step 1 in nervous-system whispering is becoming aware of our own bodily responses: they give us vital information about the other's experience of being in the world – in Lucca's case, of dullness and lack of spark.

When I, or indeed anyone, tried to offer Lucca empathy or

emotional interest, it was met with blankness. He was not deliberately ignoring us, although I am sure many, including his parents, siblings, and teachers, felt that he was. Rather, his early experiences meant that the world he predicted, his priors, did not include minds being interested in him. My words were like paint brushed onto a dusty and unprepared surface; they were never going to stick.

Lucca in nursery had been described as 'good' and 'quiet', a description often heard with such worrying cut-off presentations. Physically he reached the usual milestones, but he demanded little emotionally from others and received little back, giving rise to a kind of numbness-enhancing feedback loop.

I organised an observation in his classroom and saw that he was left on his own too much, while staff gave attention to more demanding children. We met with school staff to help them understand him, especially the fact that, having been starved of early good attention, he emitted only subtle, faint, easily missed signals of desire for interaction.

In family meetings I asked the parents to spend regular one-to-one time with him, to actively follow and comment on his play, and to try to find, or inject, some energy and enthusiasm into interactions. This was hard, as his siblings naturally got most of the attention. His parents were asked to video brief interactions, and we then looked at these together, allowing us to spot hopeful signs. In one the mother was playing with a toy, and, on the video, she noticed what she had not seen at the time: Lucca fleetingly looking up at her with what was unmistakably enjoyment. Another was when his mother had to get up and leave the room, and, when she returned, he looked up and his body relaxed. These were little clues that he needed her and wanted to be in her company. Such clues gave his mother hope and courage to persevere, leaving her feeling more needed, more wanted, more like a mum.

School staff were helped to encourage him out of his shell and were surprised at his ability to engage. In family sessions any hint of a more interactive gesture, any showing of desire or interest, was hammed up and amplified. The model I used here and with similar cases comes from seminal work by Selma Fraiberg in the 1960s with blind babies and sighted mothers.[29] At that time, blind babies were often institutionalised and could be confused with autistic children, rocking and self-soothing and not expecting interaction. Fraiberg helped these mothers draw their infants into an interpersonal world by pointing out easily missed signs. While their faces might not have lit up in response to their mother's voices, a little toe wiggle here and hand gesture there were clear indications that their mothers were important to them. This encouraged the mothers to interact more, and the babies in turn responded, becoming livelier and, importantly, more rewarding to look after.

This is the method we used with Lucca's parents. They now came to the clinic with stories of change. Once when he had drawn a small picture, one of his first ever, his mother asked to see it, and he showed her, and she was thrilled and showed him how pleased she was. A few days later he did another drawing and sidled up near to her, and she sensed that he was showing her his new picture. At last, here was a boy who was enjoying positive attention, was starting to expect it, and was enjoying being enjoyed. Soon they could share enjoyment of other things, perhaps a flower or an aeroplane, pointing things out to each other, an example of the important developmental milestone – intersubjectivity.

We helped his parents to become nervous-system whisperers, to translate seemingly purely physiological gestures, such as his legs jiggling or clenching his fists, into the language of emotions ('Ooh, you seem worried about that nice big dog', 'Ouch, that was a big loud noise'). Having his feelings understood allowed him to feel relief and led to him calming and then to showing interest. The sequence here was from fear and contracting to connection and feeling safe, and this resetting then leading to rebooting, including of interest and curiosity and, indeed, of his lifegiver.

Such an ability to read bodily signals and learn their significance is crucial for emotional development. If my heart races, it might mean that I am anxious, or possibly excited, and I can learn the difference, but first I must learn to recognise that my heart is racing and that this might have significance. So many people whom I am calling unsparked are cut off from a body awareness that allows them to read and respond to their own emotional signals.

Lucca, like others similar to him, had a 'damped-down' system, unlike hyperactive and acting-out children. If you are subject to danger or violence, you need to be alert, read signs in faces, be ready for defensive action. On the other hand, if you are left alone, your earliest learning, your priors, are that there is not much point in expecting much from others. It is easy to forget that unresponsive, unrewarding kids like Lucca have become as they are because of early lives in very depriving environments where they were left to get by in ways that are almost too painful to think about.

Sparking Lucca

When with people like Lucca, it is easy to feign interest while in truth 'going-through-the-motions'. I am not sure that Lucca, before we met, had felt that life could be anything other than a 'going-through-the-motions'. Sometimes he would indulge in dull, self-soothing activities, like bouncing a ball for ages. When I realised this was not helpful, I intervened actively, such as by making this into something more interpersonal. I would jump in, reach the ball, bounce it myself, and signal for him to make the next bounce, a reciprocal two-person game replacing a solitary self-soothing activity. Or, as he drew a robot, one that he had done many times and I was bored with, I playfully made my own mark on the page. He looked at me, a bit annoyed and nonplussed. I looked back at him and then at the page, beckoning him to join in. He responded to my marks with his own, and again something akin to a mutual turn-taking game developed. This, of course, was a trick learnt from Donald Winnicott's 'squiggle' technique,[30] which long ago was so successful with his child patients. These were ways of hauling Lucca out of his solipsistic world into human emotional connection.

Slowly games developed, both at home and in therapy, such as hide-and-seek and peekaboo, both of which are often seen in the play of children who have had major separations. Lucca initially would just smile, sometimes laugh, and by the end screech with pleasure when found, expecting, wanting, and even demanding attention. As Donald Winnicott once said, 'it is a joy to be hidden but disaster not to be found'.[31] At last, Lucca was being actively looked for, was really enjoying being found, and he too was seeking and finding. This was the beginning of agency, sparking, of a lifegiver growing. It was as if his system, which had shut down from early danger and lack of nourishment, had been rebooted, allowing spark-inducing connections to be made.

People like Lucca know little about positive emotions such

as enjoyment, excitement, liveliness, or joy. Their priors do not include a belief in pleasurable interactions. Such undrawn children have not developed the agency and confidence that grows from attuned, playful interactions. Infancy research describes how babies love making things happen, whether making a noise by pulling a cord, of making mother come with shouting.[7] When all goes well, babies are active participants in social life from the off. Neglected children like Lucca rarely develop this enjoyable sense of their own agency. Such a zest for life, our seeking system,[32] only sparks up when we feel safe. Then, like Lucca, we see the emergence of a lifegiver seeking pleasure, exploration, and a more 'outgoing' way of being.

For us to develop an interest in life, someone must have been interested in us, something that neglected children generally lacked. When Lucca would smile, even slightly, or seem excited, I would try to meet that feeling, maybe with an 'Oh yes, that is exciting.' The trick was being alive to faint signs of life, which is hard if one has already been lulled into deadness. I worry about the signs that bypassed me over the years. When such small signs of life are amplified, we can build animated interpersonal exchanges. With Lucca, by the end we often enjoyed each other, and he was becoming livelier, and more open.

Within a year he was remarkably transformed, so much so that he was getting into trouble in school and his parents even worried that he was getting too rowdy! The boy whom nobody had previously noticed had begun to expect and even demand attention, was being a rival with his siblings, was noisy when ignored, and was definitely someone who knew that he had needs and was able to express them. At the point of referral, the parents had felt that they had made a big mistake in adopting

Lucca. Initially he certainly did not inspire affection, love, or pleasure, but now his parents felt a deep love and passion for Lucca, and they definitely were not going to let him go.

The work with Lucca was easier than with many cases, as he was young, with much developmental potential that we could nurture. Nonetheless, this story could easily have ended up differently, and the lively sparky little boy who was beginning to emerge from his deadened states could definitely have missed out on his life-enhancing resparking journey.

Explaining Lucca's development

Some people do not experience the conditions that allow healthy sparking to flourish. If, like Lucca, one languishes in a neglectful orphanage and lacks love, attunement, or emotional understanding, one has little choice but to withdraw and become less emotionally alive. It is almost too painful to imagine that infants, born primed for human interaction, care, and love, could be left alone with so little human contact. Children like Lucca are extreme examples, but over the years I worked with many others adopted from similarly appalling circumstances.

We do, though, see milder versions of such turning inwards in all of us. Even the happiest, best-cared-for babies can get anxious and close down when, for example, a parent withdraws, even temporarily. Then often their body states become disorganised, and they can stare and go into glazed, given-up states. They recover quickly, as most of us do: we re-find spark that was previously there. Not so infants and children whose neglect was more ongoing, and whose beings lack an embodied memory of good experiences that can be returned to.

Although I have started with an example of extreme neglect, similar lessons can be applied to most of us in dulled, given-up states. Even very desparked people like Lucca can, with the right input, 'warm up', get livelier, and start to spark. We all can. We often need help to believe that we can have an impact, leave a mark. If we are lucky, we learn about making an impact when we are responded to as infants, when a parent shows sympathy for a baby's upset or beams a smile in response to a grin. Especially if there has previously been some spark, we can generally find a way to rekindle interest, agency, and enjoyment.

What any of us require in such states is similar. We need, first, to be understood for who we are and for what we are experiencing. Just trying to chivvy someone into cheerfulness never works. Feeling understood, as with Lucca, gives rise to a sense of connection with another, and a feeling of safeness. After such a safening and reset, we see mood shifts, kindling of sparks, a lifegiver coming to the fore.

To help anyone to open up to their feelings, we need a finely tuned radar, a nervous-system sensor, that can pick up faint sparks of potential life. With Lucca, this happened when I spotted him showing need for his mother, which brought her to tears. With all those I have worked with, they need first to feel safe but then be 'safely' pushed outside their comfort zone. By the end he was demanding attention in boisterous ways, attention he did not even know existed when we started. He jumped out in hide-and-seek, shouted when he was ignored, and knew how to get what he needed. With his rise in energy we saw bodily changes, increased muscle tone, less floppiness, greater pulsing with life and vibrancy. He had needed help to become a bit of a loveable rascal.

The risk when we do not succeed can be disastrous. Early

numbing, whether in neglect or of a milder kind, such as after withdrawn maternal depression,[33] leads to being less exploratory, showing less empathy, and being more passive and withdrawn, resulting in poorer cognitive outcomes. Neglect is deadening and often has a worse trajectory than overt trauma, albeit more silently deadly. People can become what the psychoanalyst Christopher Bollas called 'normotic', psychologically 'unborn', often emotionless.[34] The feelings they often struggle with are not pain or upset, but positive ones, such as excitement, joy, pleasure, or desire.

Their initial deprivation, such as neglect, can lead to what the child psychotherapist Gianna Henry calls 'double-deprivation',[35] a second deprivation of tragically not being able to recognise kindness or care that is available. It is hard but so very important to find passion for neglected states, for children sitting in the back of class unnoticed, for adult wallflowers being overlooked – as well as, of course, for the dulled-down, lifeless parts of ourselves. Desparking too easily goes unnoticed. I always feel hopeful when the unnoticed ones become demanding and a bit rascally. I was a shy boy too and know how much I needed to be energised; I am forever grateful to the few teachers and friends who spotted my withdrawal and did not let me slip away. I know too well both the fear of enlivening and the thrilling, tingling excitement when it happens.

When things go well, minds, especially young ones, form and grow in response to attuned emotionally sensitive caregiving. Babies need to feel loved and enjoyed, as we all do, and need to have their difficult feelings understood. The world feels very different when we feel 'held-in-mind' by people who understand us. Lucca's flattened, unsparked states arose through the lack of good reciprocal experiences, which ideally are incrementally built up over the early seconds, minutes, hours, and then days, weeks, months, and years of a young life. We all need what Colwyn Trevarthen[27] calls a 'companion in meaning making': another person who with empathy and curiosity can help us be safely and enjoyably in the world. Lucca, luckily, was young enough to respond to his new companions in meaning-making, which in time metamorphosed into an internal companion in meaning-making and a lifegiver.

CHAPTER 7
RESPARKING FROM DEADNESS

Damped and damping

A lack of spark occurs for understandable reasons. Most of us know this in small ways, such as how, when let down by someone, we can feel flat or low. This is greatly exacerbated in people who have too few good experiences over a long period time. Young brains are incredibly flexible, and fledgling humans adapt to fit into whatever environment they happen to be born into. If reading other people's emotions is not useful in an environment, such as in Lucca's depriving orphanage, then different brain pathways will develop to those seen in a child who has been lovingly interacted with,[28] or one who has been subjected to violence. For example, the amygdala, which is generally implicated in brain circuitries central to emotionality, fires up more slowly in neglected children when they are shown a picture of an angry face, than it does in most children; while those exposed to violence show much speedier reactivity in the same brain regions.[36] That makes sense: if we have often experienced violence, it is crucial to recognise warning signs and react swiftly; whereas if we are isolated in a cot, there is less reason to worry about such danger.

In neglect, brain circuitry central to recognising emotions is less online. An implication of this is that, when with someone who is not in touch with my feelings or thoughts, I will feel less motivated to interact with them. I might also unwittingly resonate with them, taking on something of their dulled psychological state. Indeed, researchers found that just hearing a discourse that has an avoidant, cut-off style leads listeners to be less emotionally available and more socially aversive with other people for some time afterwards[37] – a powerful finding.

Any of us can be not only un-sparked, but also de-sparking – both damped down but also damping of others. It has been one of the hardest things in my career to keep emotionally alive and present, to find hope, compassion, and passion, in the presence of such damping force fields.

Resparking after being emotionally cut-off: Rosemary

I felt a deep *ennui* in the early months of Rosemary's therapy, a dread, a knot in my stomach, breath shallow, a lack of energy. This makes sense, given her story. Now in her thirties, as a 6-year-old, Rosemary had witnessed her younger sister shockingly run over and killed outside her home. Her parents had partly blamed her but also felt extremely guilty themselves.

Both parents became depressed, the mother suicidal and requiring hospitalisation intermittently, the father disappearing into work and opiate dependence. After her sister's death, Rosemary did not receive the compassionate care, loving attention, or lively encouragement that she needed in order for her to thrive. The parents became overprotective: she was kept away from friends and barely allowed out of the house; extracurricular activities were banned, and she was often kept at home during school, possibly as an emotional prop for her mother. By the time we met, her life was very constricted, living alone, working in a dull administrative job, with no real friends, spending most of her time in a reclusive semi-numb state. She had tried therapists before, but either she, or her therapists, had quickly given up.

It was Rosemary's pallor and lack of aliveness in her body that first struck me. The paleness, I suspect, was exacerbated by her lack of sunlight or physical activity, on top of her history of emotional shut-down. At the time of the tragedy and afterwards, her parents could not reach out to where she was emotionally, could not help Rosemary or themselves face the awful feelings they were all living with. She needed help to mourn, to, in time, move on and become an alive person. She, of course, felt guilty about having any life, a classic symptom of survivor guilt, feeling bad if she experienced hope, pleasure, enjoyment, a future. It was as if she was in a time-warp, stuck in unprocessed guilt, grief, and trauma.

In my room she would sit still, disappearing into her chair, mouse-like and mostly silent, occasionally speaking in a monotone if prompted. I tried to offer quiet interest, concern, and empathy and to cultivate safeness. Very occasionally she would make eye contact. Her words were few. Sometimes she would just stop and withdraw into a deep unreachable state, staring, almost catatonic, not responding to me. I felt I had to be very vigilant lest she slip into a dark, unreachable state.

I began to dread these withdrawals. When I noticed them begin, I felt shivers of horror. One day, spontaneously, as I saw this about to happen, I uncharacteristically screamed 'No', with urgency. This desperate alert was enough to help Rosemary return to the present, in effect to come into some aliveness with me, into connectedness. She needed someone, unlike her parents, to believe in her ability to live a fuller life, to have and process feelings with her, to reach out and draw her out of her frozen dark pit. There were many occasions when I needed to actively haul her out of such bleak holes.

It was, I believe, my determination to connect that, over time, allowed Rosemary to make progress. She had gone underground after the accident, after which she desparked, lights that had been on going out. But layers of her personality were unsparked – that is, never sparked – as she had not had the loving, caring, mutually rewarding relationships to enable her potentials to come fully alive.

The death, alongside overprotective parenting, led her into a withdrawn semi-dissociative state where she got stuck, a stuck-ness reminiscent of cell danger response. Rosemary needed to be fought for, to be 'reclaimed', as Anne Alvarez called it,[38] to be actively brought back to life. My active approach was an attempt at resuscitation, a necessary precursor of getting to know and trust safeness, and eventually for healthy sparking. It was a struggle to get the right balance between empathy – in her case, for the unthinkable states she went into – and hope, the belief that relationships could bring her back to life. I needed to experiment with how deep to go into her dark, airless ditch, and how far to stay outside it and beckon her into the light.

Sparking into connection

The calling of Rosemary back into relationship was just the start of our work. She had many 'deactivated' personality characteristics common in people whose parents could not tolerate emotions. This made her a challenge to work with. Often, I felt a bit spaced out with her. In fact, I was surprised that she had come to therapy.

Her stated reason was feeling empty, which at least gave me hope that she knew something was wrong.

Rosemary was thin, quiet, and distant, her body held in, skin colourless, with flaccid muscle tone, and eyes lacking sparkle. The muscles around her eyes, the orbicularis oculi, which connect with the important ventral vagal nerve pathways central to emotional life,[39] revealed a lack of aliveness – often a bad sign. Despite her politeness, her manner was often subtly dismissive of my concern. When I would try to think about something that might have been bothering her, maybe a work problem, she would mostly just shrug, or occasionally say things like, 'You just have to get on with it.' This was possibly typical of the unempathic messages she received from her parents.

She started each session with a placatory smile and would rely on me to initiate conversation, otherwise silence ensued. If I asked about her week, she might blandly recount a few events. When I tried to open things up, I felt parried, as she insisted there was nothing to tell. I took to being more forceful. 'Come on, Rosemary', I might say, 'you can do better than that. I really want to hear, perhaps you don't believe that?' She could then at least look at me in response, and sometimes smile.

When young, she had learnt that feelings were not to be talked about, that they were best avoided. I noted how hard it is to come into this strange world called therapy. I asked, 'How do you feel when you are sitting here, like now?' She had no answer, looking nonplussed. I asked aloud, 'Do you feel nervous, worried, angry, embarrassed, I wonder, perhaps put your thumb up if I am anywhere near, or down if I am dead wrong.' She laughed, I said, 'Go on then', and we had a game to play, but she was enjoying my interest and getting more interested in herself.

In another session, after she yet again evasively said that she was fine, I suggested that she would probably say she was fine if the world was about to be blown up. She laughed, her laughter a hopeful signal of play and connection, and colour came to her cheeks. In such interactions some genuine contact was being made, connection that could be the basis for resetting and resparking. Developing trust, some belief in feeling safe, in relationships, in others' interest in her, were my aims at this stage. For a long time, I kept away from talking about the trauma. That would have been too much at this point, too early, as she as yet lacked the equipment to process difficult memories; indeed, talking about and facing them prematurely might have sent her back into a shut-down world.

From safening to mourning

Therapy was starting to have an impact. I began to ask Rosemary about her bodily feelings, such as whether she noticed when she was holding her breath, or if the slight tensing of her jaw or kicking of her feet might be telling us something. These were early stages of nervous-system whispering. I said, 'I am not surprised this feels difficult; you have had a lifetime of not feeling feelings. I know there was little room for difficult feelings in your family, they were an alien, annoying interference.' She sighed in relief, and her face looked sad.

After a typical avoidant reply to a question, I said, with as much feeling as I could muster, 'You really can't believe that I'm interested in you, can you?' Some emotion ran across her face; she was touched. I said again, 'Feelings are a bit of a foreign country, especially the idea that yours might be important and of interest, to me, to anyone.' She looked at me and away, out of her comfort zone. I again noted a hint of sadness, of real feeling.

Such moments of sadness did allow us to begin to do more of the painful work of processing the death of her sister, to start to go over the shock, the horror, the pain, the incredulity. We also had to face the upsetting realisation of how difficult her parents had found giving her what she had needed emotionally. She, in time, could mourn some of the few lovely qualities of her sister that she could remember, and also mourn the loss of the sister she should have had growing up.

Slowly Rosemary began to trust that I could be there for her. It was like a process of thawing out, of loosening and softening. Under the icy defences were multiple layers of deep pain. Once trust was established, she felt safe enough to experience and process this. Many sessions were spent in agonising tears, but this was hopeful, and an idea was growing that life could have been different, and still could be.

A lifegiver appears

After several months of this kind of work, something shifted. It was as if there had been a sufficiently replenishing reset for her lifegiver to appear. She told me that she wanted her life to change, that she could not make friends as she was so unconfident, that people did not seem interested in her. Nervously she confided that no men seemed to like her. I noted not just the upset, but also that a part of her wanted something more.

In forthcoming weeks, I saw further shifts. She looked me in the eye on arrival. When I probed and showed interest, she could tell me about things that were upsetting her, such as at work. If she breathed more deeply, a sigh, I took heart, as this was a signal of striated muscle tension, indicating that she was having feelings that might be accessed. She told me how, at work, when colleagues asked who was coming for a drink, she always felt rooted to the spot, paralysed. After many weeks she found the courage to say that she would like to join them. Expecting rejection, instead she was welcomed, her priors healthily challenged and confounded.

She was able to tell me about her obsessional tendencies, such as her need to keep everything super-tidy – not uncommon in shut-down people who use routines to hold themselves together. I talked about her fear of messiness, including messy feelings. Her mother, too, hated mess. She dropped a tissue to the floor and quickly picked it up. I suggested that, instead, she might deliberately drop some more, and soon there was a game in which she was throwing tissues, paper, and pens across my room. This was not destructive or aggressive, although I often felt that she would benefit from being a bit aggressive. She was learning to feel a sense of agency, to throw some caution to the wind, to be childlike, playful, to feel more alive – in effect, she was starting to spark.

A few months later, she told me that she wanted to go dancing and had started to dance at home to music. She looked shy, almost shamefaced. I said how brilliant I thought that was. I felt like a dad encouraging a shy toddler to be expressive and asked if she might dare show me. She looked awkward, but there was a hint of muscular charge, faster breathing, colour in her face, all hopeful signs of energy and striated muscle tension. I asked what music she liked to dance to. She told me, and I encouraged her to play some on her phone. As she did so, I moved my shoulders and head appreciatively, deliberately being a bit gawky, and she laughed, and we both smiled. She joined in, and we were having fun. More importantly, I knew she was enjoying me enjoying her, an experience the young Rosemary had so badly lacked.

Pushing past comfort zones

While a lot of therapy is about processing pain, sadness, and anxiety, and this was the case for Rosemary too, she also needed to learn that, in life, there could be pleasure, fun, and mutual enjoyment.

Sometimes it helps to 'fake it to make it', as Amy Cuddy's work has taught us. Trying out new gestures can change our mood, and how we are perceived. Cuddy suggested that when women take on what she called 'power poses', they feel more powerful and in turn are taken more seriously.[40] Research shows that taking a contracted as opposed to an open posture is linked to depressed feelings and poor self-esteem,[41] the opposite of zest.

One famous psychoanalyst, Michael Balint, described a talented patient who always let herself down. She was bright but failed her exams, lively and sociable but could not manage relationships. She had learnt to keep her feet firmly planted on the ground and said to Balint that, despite wishing to, she had never managed to do a somersault. His famous response was, 'What about it now?' At this point she got up and somersaulted across the room. Balint described this as a 'new beginning', after which 'many changes followed in her emotional, social, and professional life, all towards greater freedom and elasticity'.[42] We were seeing something similar with Rosemary, who was slowly developing a soft front but also a bit of a wild heart!

By the end of our work, I had come to like her, and also care about her. I hardly ever felt bored in sessions any more. She rarely seemed about to disappear, and when she looked like she might, she was easily pulled back now. She had had a new experience of being with someone who could bear her pain and despair and also both enjoy her and be interested in her range of emotional states. She now had a capacity for emotionally alive and engaged interaction and definitely had spark, life-force, an incipient lifegiver.

Rosemary had had a double whammy. The trauma had led to a retreat, a dissociative numbing, a desparking, the lights almost going out, a hope-crushing deadening. In addition, her innate potential to become emotionally alive was stunted due to her not being understood, shown interest in, or enjoyed. She had consequently withdrawn, which is common in people with more dismissing, avoidant attachment styles who tend to show brain activity suggesting a tendency to avoid rather than approach others, and to be less aroused by emotional stimuli.[43]

Rosemary had, by the end, developed more tone in her body and more aliveness. She had also started to look attractive and, to her surprise, was winning admirers. She could now move towards experience, not avoid it, all with a strong back and a softer, more open, even wild, heart, and her expectations, her priors, were changing.

Rosemary's progress followed a common pattern. I had to become aware of the stultifying and deadening world she lived in and bear it with her, containing it with as much capaciousness as I could muster. I had to ensure I could reach her, meet her, in her case more forcefully than is usual. I had to make sure she felt sufficiently safe and trusting to allow softening, to become curious, about me, her feelings, the world of emotions. Only then could the work of mourning begin to take place. After that process, which I think of as a kind of reset, it was possible to reboot and stimulate her appetite, drive, hope, spark, and enjoyment.

CHAPTER 8
SPECTRUMS AND PROTECTIVE SHELLS

Danger spectrum

Children with autism, often described as having spectrum disorder (ASD), may show similar characteristics to others I have written about in this book. Like traumatised children, they can easily be overwhelmed by loud noises, leading to a withdrawal in the face of sensory overload. They then can retreat into repetitive and addictive activities, such as counting, spinning, rocking, or flapping. In effect, they are closing down against danger signals. Robert Naviaux,[3] who first described the cell danger response, found in exciting new research that drugs that turn off cell danger signalling in the body can help people on the spectrum lose many of their symptoms. Similarly, interventions that help such children manage sensations rather than be overwhelmed by them, such as Sensory Integration Therapy, can help them feel safe and live with more ease. The ritualistic behaviours, the flapping, the repetitive activities, are often ways of holding oneself together out of a kind of fear, a closing down to an experience of threat. We all do this in milder ways, of course – in my case, as a child, for example, tie sucking, repetitive games, and counting steps as I walked.

We see something similar in many of us who have thin skins,

something that is common in traumatised people. If we have not internalised a sufficiently capacious container able to process complex emotional experiences, then when triggered by a threatening stimulus, such as a loud voice or an unexpected situation, it is common to feel overwhelmed and to defend against this by shutting down. Frances Tustin, who pioneered child psychotherapy with autistic children,[44] suggested that many children on the spectrum develop what she called protective shells, what some have described as an exoskeleton or hard carapace, to shield them from sensations that are too much to bear. These understandable responses are a form of defensive numbing, a bit like a fuse blowing when an electrical circuit is at risk of running amok.

When with adults and children on the spectrum, I have sometimes felt a similar *ennui* to that experienced when working with neglect, tiredness, feeling less alive and sparked. Again, the science makes some sense of this. While most neurotypical people use a different part of the brain when looking at human faces from that for looking at inanimate objects, many on the spectrum use similar brain circuitry for looking at both faces and objects.[45] In other words, sometimes such children and adults see and treat people like objects – not callously or deliberately, but just because that is how their brains are wired. This is not easy for those of us who want people to understand our social cues and be interested in our thoughts, desires, and motivations.

Neurotypicality alongside ASD

Anne Alvarez has suggested we help identify and build non-autistic parts of the personality in children on the autistic spectrum. There is a risk in that suggestion of seeing autism as a pathology, to be contrasted with healthier neurotypicality. This is unhelpful and underestimates the gifts of so many on the spectrum and how interesting it can be to be with them. However, my experience is that many on the spectrum are bewildered by the neurotypical world and want to learn how to participate in it more. So perhaps a safer way of thinking about this is that we are trying to build neurodiversity, which does include finding and growing non-autistic neurotypical potentials alongside the autistic ones that we must also value.

An autistic child who is spinning or flapping their hands in a solipsistic withdrawn state can be drawn back into the interpersonal world by, for example, turning the spinning into a gentle game.

One child on the autistic spectrum, Marvin, was often flapping his hands. When I came close and gently looked him in the eye, breathed deeply and touched his hand for a moment, saying I would keep him safe, he could stop flapping. A momentary sense of safeness allowed his danger signals to reduce, enabling a softening and a connection with me.

Another former orphanage child would retreat into hunched rocking. I would sit opposite him, gently rocking in a similar rhythm. In time he noticed this, allowed it, and seemed to like it. We turned it into a game. He would be rocking, and his pace would change, and I would imitate his rhythm and pace. In fact, physical synchrony between people is linked to brain and heart-rate synchrony and feeling good about being together. I then took the lead and slowed the pace, and in turn he followed that, and it became a fun activity, sparking connection and life. His rocking, which had started as a defensive, solipsistic way of managing sensory overload, was transformed into a joint interpersonal activity with another person who provided safety and with whom he could actively interact, and even have fun. We generally see the same sequence. We must first develop safening and connection, providing a reset that sows the seeds for taking agency, initiating interactions, which together open up the possibility of a lifegiver sparking into being.

People on the autistic spectrum are not the most obvious candidates for the category of unsparked. Indeed, there are so many varieties of autism that they barely constitute a category, or, as one person apparently said, 'Once you've seen one person with autism, you've seen one person with autism'! However, many on the spectrum share similarities with other unsparked people and can serve as a useful example of how to use the thinking in this book with a wider range of people. Desparking is a way of closing down connection and defending against threat, which is what we also often see in such children and adults.

For many, including some on the spectrum, the experience of being in the world is overwhelming, and they develop multiple ways of defending against this. Frances Tustin pointed out that many autistic children carry around hard objects, like a toy car or a stone, that they hold tightly onto. They are clung to not because they have any symbolic meaning, but because such objects can give a physical sense of being held together, offering some respite from feeling unintegrated.

At the heart of this is a kind of terror, a dread of 'falling forever' or 'liquefying'.[44] Many behaviours, whether rocking, flapping, self-stroking, holding hard objects, or even doing puzzles, can be used to stave off overwhelm or danger. It is emotional safeness via empathic connection that allows these defences to be let go of.

Many of us have, or have had, habits that fall into this

category. For some of us, it is obsessional neatness or having everything in order. Many people who know me really wish that obsessional orderliness was one of my rituals; sadly it is not, but I have many other annoying ones! My interest in autism stemmed from my own early overwhelm. I know now how much I needed safening and contact with a compassionate, kind, understanding adult when at 9 years of age I was alone in boarding school, acting strangely. We all sometimes use mechanisms to numb down and despark, to manage what feels too much. However, we need help to come out of these places, otherwise it has dire repercussions for the likelihood of living a life rich in rewarding relationships and pleasurable experiences.

Unsparked and misfiring: Mikel

Eight-year-old Mikel definitely was both unsparked and unsparking, but he was hard to put into a clear category. He had been dragged to umpteen assessments, tests, and scans but remained a puzzle to paediatricians, psychiatrists, and multiple professionals. He was eventually given an autistic spectrum diagnosis, which might or might not have been correct but was possibly a way of making some sense of him and getting medical input. He was strange to look at: his head seeming unconnected to his body; he moved oddly, almost dragging his feet, often making bizarre gestures, avoiding eye contact, living in his own head rather than the interpersonal world that makes life worth living for most of us.

He was the younger of two boys. The older boy had been a very unhappy baby, constantly crying and hard to soothe. Mikel was born 6 weeks premature and was described as 'good', a label that often worries me. I imagine that after his parents' struggles with parenting their firstborn, it was a huge relief to have a quiet baby. As a result, however, he was barely interacted with. The fact that no one had any real memory of his infancy increased my worry; I had the feeling that he had never been properly thought about. He also had hearing issues, so he would have struggled to understand his parents or others, and his poor hearing probably left him living in a kind of muffled world anyway. His auditory problems were only treated at the age of 4 years, by which time they would have taken a terrible toll.

His parents divorced soon after his birth. His mother was lively, busy, and had been desperate to leave the marriage. His father was an IT engineer, a very logical man, who lived in his head and was hard to engage; he was fragile, nervous, and shy, with underlying psychiatric issues; he had a breakdown after the divorce. Father's father had been murdered in their country of origin, and Mikel's father had seen the body. There was serious trauma in the background, but it was never spoken about.

Let's imagine the impact of Mikel's early life. Catapulted prematurely from his mother's body many weeks earlier than humans evolved to survive, he was placed in incubators, and, instead of loving care, he experienced bright lights, constant changes of nurses, needles in his feet and arms, disconcerting sounds, indeed nothing that might have led him to feel safe. He should have been acclimatising to his parents' touch, the feel of their skin, be regulated by their body temperature, heartbeat, and breathing, soothed by their voices, their smell, his mother's breast, in effect calmed by loving presence. Way before his mind was able to sense this, he was experiencing danger signals rather than safeness-enhancing ones. Danger signals give rise to closing down and disconnecting, and Mikel had had to cut off feeling, to turn in and away, hence the staring into space, self-touching, and rocking to soothe himself.

He was left on his own, his mother depressed and regretful of the birth, his father cut-off and despairing. He missed out on what babies thrive on – loving interaction, seeing eyes lit up by his presence, preverbal playful interchanges, smiling and being smiled at and laughed with. Thus, he had not learnt the toolset to join in the social world. He barely interacted with other children in nursery or school, and at best he could demand attention by annoyingly shouting or doing odd things.

The work of resparking

I did not find Mikel easy to be with. He had a range of rituals – strange gestures, rubbing his hands, tapping his feet, rocking, grunting – and would suck on his clothes, a self-soothing gesture for which my personal history gave me a modicum of sympathy. His clothes always looked the wrong size, his trousers short, his legs dangling, shirt dishevelled. I dreaded sessions, as they contained so little life.

His voice was a drawl and hard to understand, slow and stilted – perhaps not surprising, given how he was simply not spoken or listened to much as an infant. He had no preconception of listeners alert to and interested in his thoughts. In addition, his hearing issues would have precluded responding to voices and other sounds. Instead of playing imaginatively, he indulged in repetitive activities with toys. I tried my best to engage him, to show interest, to be active and think about his mind, his feelings, and what he might be experiencing. I worked hard to retain some aliveness, to not give up, to watch for hopeful moments. When his half hint of a smile felt a tiny bit more real, I would amplify it; or when he showed a modicum of interest in something, I would try to show pleasure in his gesture. It was an effort, though – I was definitely faking it to make it!

I remember that some months in, to my surprise, he began to enact something that seemed like a game. There was a shop, I deciphered through his drawl, and he was a shopkeeper, and I was supposed to buy things that he put out on a table. It was rudimentary, lifeless, and I found it hard to stay interested. When I went to his shop, often there was nothing to buy, and I was left frustrated. He would ask me to answer a pretend phone-call and then leave me in silence. I often wondered if I was getting an experience rather like he had as an infant, the waiting, silence, nothing coming back, experiencing a void where interested, attuned mutual attention should have led to a mind and heart growing.

I talked aloud about what I imagined his experience to be, what it might feel like to be faced with silence and unpredictability, how unnerving I knew that can feel. In time, he showed interest in my reflections, my attempts to process feelings he might have had but would not consciously have known he had. He clearly liked this as, after a while, he would up the ante, actively enjoying making me feel that deadly 'waiting for Godot'[46] feeling. He was becoming interested in seeing his experience processed by me, talked about, and reflected back at him. It helped him to feel more real and understood, more contained.

One day he drew a tree, and it had absolutely no roots, like it was floating. I thought this was how he felt in the world, with no core, solidity, or depth. Most of the time I felt dispirited, in a kind of haze myself, fearing I was making no progress. To me he seemed the same every session, repetitive and uninteresting, but I would force myself to try to make sense of him, to stay psychologically alive.

In time, there were developments. His play included more characters, many of whom could not be trusted. Scenes took place where I was to trust someone, possibly a policeman or customer, and then be told that I had been tricked and they were impostors. While it is true that it was his first symbolic and imaginative play, and in retrospect I might have felt pleased, in fact I felt like I was walking in a quagmire.

Occasionally I saw hopeful developments. I would talk loudly from the feeling-state I imagined he might have experienced, saying things like, 'It feels so upsetting to be tricked, a horrible feeling', and, later, 'I feel very angry that I was tricked, it's just not fair' as I banged the table. At this he looked up, as if interested in the idea that a person could be angry, that there was this feeling that someone could experience, express, and name. Anger is a hopeful feeling for kids like Mikel; it suggests some faith in something better. Here were faint signs of desire, of agency, even spark, of the kindling of a lifegiver.

He would also show me he did not want sessions to end by turning the clock upside down! That allowed me to talk in a pretend cross way about how upset he was about me stopping before he was ready. Voicing his feelings, I said forcefully, 'That's just not fair, Mr Music, I am cross you are stopping the session.' This led him to look me in the eye, and then smile, a smile of pleasure. In time, he would also smile when he first saw me, walk a little more eagerly to the session, almost a skip in his step, but if I were honest, I was not noting much change. Surprisingly, though, after about eight months, school reported that he was doing better, he had stopped chewing his clothes, was interacting more with other children, and his grades had improved. I was flabbergasted. I was not sure I could trust this change; it felt shaky, but perhaps that was me experiencing something of his lack of trust and hope.

Mikel had withdrawn into his own world very early. His prematurity and being left alone was compounded by his hearing issues and, further, by warring parents who had little appetite for parenting and whose attention mostly went to his brother. Infants can be described as 'contingency detectors', looking out for what has an effect, watching how a parent responds to their gestures such as smiles or cries. If they do not get a response, they tend to turn away and inwards, and much more so if this giving up is in the early months. Such turning away is particularly common in premature babies. It is experiences of emotional connection, like mutual gazing, facial mirroring, rhythmic verbal and gestural exchanges, that facilitate an infant to feel safe, to soften, to turn towards, not away, to open to hope with a softer front instead of withdrawing from the interpersonal world.

Mikel's time with me was, sadly, probably his first experience of someone really trying to attune to him. What I did, and what we encouraged his teachers and parents to do, eventually paid dividends. As with Rosemary, he needed to be called back into life, or possibly be drawn into it for the first time. As Anne Alvarez suggested, withdrawn people do not need complex psychological understanding; rather, they need a 'Hey', a 'Look, there is life here, you can have some, you can join in.'[26] Mikel, like all of us at times, definitely needed an active 'hey', a calling back to life, like the fabled kiss that awakens so many fairy-tale characters from slumber.

I imagine Mikel would always have a bit of strangeness about him, but he was becoming more like other boys. He seemed increasingly in his body, his clothes almost fitting, walking straighter, looking ahead more, holding eye-contact, and, for the first time, having some friends in school. While his prognosis was uncertain, he had become a different and even likeable boy.

PART IV

Mis-sparking: the wrong kind of sparking

CHAPTER 9
DESIRE, AND ADDICTIVE BUZZ TRAPS

The first desire

Straight after birth, a new baby, when placed on its mother's tummy, can slowly crawl towards the breast, sometimes pausing en route to look into her eyes, and on arriving can latch on and suck, albeit often needing help. Irrespective of crawling to a breast or even having a mother, the earliest desires and drivers of humans are always for connection, relationship, and emotional contact. From these first moments of life, we see desire, a psychobiological life-force, a propelling of oneself towards emotional connection.

Life would be poorer without such desire, without an appetitive or seeking system,[32] which drives us towards what we want, whether food, sex, or other good experiences. What stimulates most desire and reward from infancy onwards is the desire for relationship – indeed, this should be the primary driver for most people throughout life. This is not the case for many unsparked people who have turned inwards, resorting to contracting and self-soothing, turning away from connection. They then have less life-force and desire, are less able to turn towards their lifegiver, and can withdraw into an insulated, anti-hope stance.

I suggest that what triggers most addictions are unmanageable feelings, and the root of these is a history of lacking good emotional connection. Addictions are one way to numb, contract, avoid pain and difficult feelings that we wish to escape from. I have for many years worked with people struggling with different addictions, from alcohol, drugs, compulsive shopping, food, and, more recently, pornography and gaming. Each object of addiction has a different effect and is used for different reasons. However, nearly always they are reached for to compensate for the lack of good feelings inside.

We all have addictive tendencies, whether towards chocolate, cake, wine, smartphones, gaming, shopping, or whatever. My own include screens, the 'buy-it-now' button, and also things that can seem healthy, like exercise or work. We often turn to our objects of addiction when confronted by something difficult, perhaps a stressor, bad news, anxiety, rejections, work pressure. To stave off the addictive pulls, we need to find a way of bearing such difficult feelings, capaciously containing them rather than defending against them by succumbing to our addiction of choice.

Reward seeking, good and bad

Addictions piggyback on systems in the brain that are there for good reasons, are central to pleasure or reward seeking, and have served us well in evolutionary history. For example, they drive us towards food and sex, without which our species could not reproduce and pass on our genes, and life would be far less rewarding.

Of course, throughout evolutionary history our reward-seeking systems were most active when there was a felt need. The lion does not hunt after a huge feed, and mammals, including humans, rarely seek out sex straight after a satisfying sexual encounter. If we are reasonably secure, at ease, and emotionally present, we might not be constantly seeking new rewards but will still have the confidence and flexibility to respond when a potential reward shows up. Hunter-gathers might, for example, drop everything if they realise that hunting a nutrient-rich animal or snaffling honey was a possibility.

They might also play a very long game and track an animal for hours or even days. This requires effort, motivation, and an expectation of reward at the end. In my twenties, I bought and sold antiques, and I often wondered if my bargain hunting was a bit like hunting prey, if more addictive!

Our brains learn how to seek out and find pleasure. If I have a pleasing or exciting experience, my reward circuits will probably fire up when I think about it happening again. That experience might be a child being with a loving parent, an evening somewhere where I had a romance, or a tree with honey in it. An area in the brain called the VTA (ventral tegmental area) is where much of the neurotransmitter dopamine is produced. The VTA connects to many other brain areas. So, if something is rewarding, such as climbing a tree and finding honey, this system suggests, 'Hey that felt great, let's make sure we do it again. I must remember what happened and repeat it.' The mesolimbic reward system reaches several relevant areas of brain circuitry, such as the amygdala, involved in the emotionality of an experience ('Wow, that feels amazing), the hippocampus ('Yes, I must remember this place'), the nucleus accumbens (helping to navigate to the potential reward), and the prefrontal cortex (helping to work out how to do it). After

I get the thing I desire, such as sweet honey or a loving sexual encounter, the feeling of satisfaction involves other neurotransmitters, such as prolactin, endorphins, or oxytocin, so involved in loving feelings. Such a rich and natural cocktail of positive experiences is one that, sadly, many who suffer from addictions do not experience.

If we have an inner deadness and lack of spark, we can defend against it via addictive activities. A lack of spark might be a result of neglect, learned helplessness, depression, trauma, or immediate life circumstances, but it entails a moving away from life and hope. Many addictions, as Gabor Maté, among others, suggests,[47] are attempts to fill such holes, ones often caused by trauma, but such attempts often lead our reward systems to go off-kilter.

We can try to manage addictions behaviourally, such as by cold turkey or removing the object of addiction, but that only goes so far if the conditions for emotional health are not also put in place. Such healthy conditions, of course, include satisfying human connections and a feeling of safeness, trust, and ease. Only then can a reboot lead to healthier reward-seeking – most healthily, of course, from human relationships.

Turning to addiction: Shura

Fourteen-year-old Shura was adopted at the age of 5 years into an aspirational middle-class family in the UK. However, from the beginning she seemed flat and unresponsive, turned away from life, shut down to the hope of rewards from relationships. She had spent her first years in two children's homes abroad, where she was neglected and was also exposed to inappropriate sexual stimulation.

There was no information about her biological family.

I really felt for her parents, who so wanted to make a success of parenting Shura. They later adopted a baby girl from another country who was bright, energetic, interested, loving, and enjoyable to be with. Shura, in contrast, seemed flat, her eyes empty, her face inexpressive, awkward in her body and energyless. In effect, she had little spark.

This picture fits with research on the plight of many children adopted after early neglect.[48] They consistently showed traits such as poor ability to recognise emotions, flattened affect, less capacity to give and receive loving care, a lowered predisposition for ordinary pleasure, and a turning away from social relationships.[49] Indeed, whole areas of their brains were found to be less online, something that partially improved for luckier children placed early enough into caring families.

The brain circuitry involved in reward seeking is affected by such early neglect.[50] It changes how dopaminergic neurons develop[51] and blunts connections between brain areas such as the prefrontal cortex and our mesolimbic dopaminergic reward circuitry, connections that are stronger when things have gone well early in life.[52] This makes sense. Life is more rewarding and spark-inducing if we have had, and expect to have, good experiences. As we see in other 'use-it-or-lose-it' scenarios, the social-reward circuits of neglected children like Shura are less used, and hence less online, leaving them less primed to seek out good experiences.[53]

Generally, when things go well and I have a good experience, I will remember it and do my darndest to make it happen again. Neglected children have not learnt to expect rewarding experiences. They anticipate blankness rather than the rewarding times luckier children expect and try to repeat. The orphan alone in a cot who sometimes finds a bottle in their mouth already has a very different motivational system from the already sparking new-born crawling towards the breast or smiling at an adoring parent. The biggest motivator and prize for most infants and children is loving, mutually enjoyable relationships. Neglected children such as Shura tragically lack these, and without emotional connection a shutting down occurs, one similar to the cell danger response. We then see people stuck in closed-down states, lacking hope, with less liveliness in their minds and bodies and less activity in their brain's reward pathways.

Anhedonia

Drugs and other objects of addiction can give a sense of excitement, rescuing people from desparked, damped states. We often see this in survivors of neglect, such as Shura. The object of reward, such as a drug or pornography, provides a spike, popularly called a dopamine hit. This can be exciting but is short-lived, not providing genuine satisfaction. Soon after the hit, the old feelings can return, leading to a vicious cycle of seeking.

Shura fitted this pattern. She was generally glum and dulled down and fitted the description of anhedonia: an inability to feel pleasure and seek rewards. Shura had few interests and no real friends, and my sense is that people were not drawn to her. Many struggling with anhedonia revert in challenging moments to addictions, such as drugs, excessive food consumption, or compulsive screen use.[54] These provide temporary respite from deadness – easy rewards that require little effort but ultimately do not shift the anhedonia.

Unfortunately, often the addiction of choice becomes less rewarding over time, more of it being needed to get that initial buzz – whether stronger drugs or more hard-edged pornography. Many addicts, when trying to come off their drug of addiction, experience high levels of anhedonia, and it then becomes very tempting to escape this by relapsing.

Shura spent a lot of time on social media. Because she was quiet and kept to herself, she disappeared under the radar. However, she became involved in worrying activities, such as video calls with older men, watching pornography, and being persuaded to send erotic pictures to boys at school. We do not know what was going on in her neurochemical system, but we do know that such addictive behaviour is common in anhedonic states, often used to push away emotional flatness. Possibly inappropriate early sexual exposure led to her being drawn to sexualised images and interaction; then again, we cannot know, but probably such images were more stimulating than anything else in her life and continually drew her back for more.

What helped?

Initially I had to actively help the family understand how her behaviour made sense, given her early background. It was tempting to see her listlessness and apathy as lazy, provocative, stubborn, or an affront to their parenting, even as caused by her 'bad genes', rather than being an understandable response to early neglect.

When they grasped the effects of her experiences, such as how she had long ago shut down from hope, her parents became more empathic, more able to watch for hopeful signs of potential development. Importantly, faint signals that indicated that she needed them were becoming apparent, such as how, when they went out and left her for a bit, she went to her computer or the fridge, clearly an attempt to fill an emotional hole. They learnt that she was not being bad but was expressing a need she did not know she had – in this case, missing them. Such insights were a relief to her parents. We could similarly help her teachers to see the triggers that led her to withdraw, so they could then take her withdrawals less personally and be more understanding.

In family sessions we learnt how deeply engrained Shura's patterns were, and we saw how such patterns showed up in family interactions. Shura could make no sense of someone talking about how she had withdrawn, and, in fact, she just withdrew more if they complained about it. However, she could respond when her father said how they loved it when she joined in, how they all wanted to help her to be part of family life. Feeling wanted was sparking of hope for her, a much healthier sparking than her former predilections.

They learnt to spot little clues, becoming nervous-system sensors, a hint of a move towards not away from them, a faint signal that she had been hurt. Feelings could in time be talked about rather than avoided. For example, she might have felt told off if any of us suggested that she was jealous of her sister, but her mother could talk about how jealous she herself had been as a girl, and I similarly talked about how I can feel jealous, that it was ok, in fact a sign of wanting closeness. Shura watched and took this all in, and we knew she was starting to feel understood. She began to expect to be part of weekend family games, spending less time on her own, no longer needing to be cajoled as much. Of course, she still liked being chased a bit, but who does not? We tried to ensure that both parents showed how thrilled they were that she was part of family activities.

Her confidence was already growing and took a leap forward when she was offered twice-weekly therapy. We worried that she would experience this as a sign of failure, but the earlier family work seemed to have paid off. She now believed that people wanted the best for her and, importantly, that people believed change was possible. And it was. She started slowly to make friendships in school, and her academic performance improved, in part because she was trying more, had more hope and confidence, and was less withdrawn. She was becoming more open to life, more alert; in effect, her lifegiver was sparking.

This was slow work, no miracle cure. Luckily, I could work with the parents for several years, helping them avoid the constant temptation to become frustrated and give up. Interestingly, we did little overt behavioural work about limiting internet use, although access to screens was now restricted to the living room, on view to all. What we did do was to spark other systems, those for pleasure and rewards, especially from interpersonal relationships, the ability to relax and bask in the company of people who were learning to enjoy her and even like and love her. With such hopeful shifts she had less need to resort to addictive activities.

As so often, the addiction was the symptom, not the problem, and igniting other systems rebalanced her motivations. She began to gain pleasure from the more ordinary things in life, family, then friends, and in time even her studies. She luckily also found that she had musical gifts and became an accomplished guitar player. This was helpful, allowing her to express herself, but also gain status at school and participate in group life. Shura was now sparking, and, as I have seen so often, this had been generated from mutually enjoyable, safe human relationships.

Trauma, addiction, and brains

Many who have suffered adverse childhood experiences such as trauma are drawn to addictive temptations, have less propensity for good experiences, are less likely to feel content, and are more likely to experience anhedonia. People like Shura grow up not experiencing much love and pleasure, and they compensate by addictively seeking rewards that do not deliver real satisfaction. Indeed, tech and gaming companies are expert at keeping us online and stimulating desires for rewards. Getting 'Likes' and new 'Friends' on Facebook overstimulates dopaminergic areas of the brain such as the nucleus accumbens but does not provide real satisfaction.[55]

Shura was typical of those who unconsciously are in the grip of an addiction. In decades-old experiments, electrodes were connected to a rat's reward circuitry.[56] The rats could stimulate that area by pulling a lever, and they did so almost constantly, over 2,000 times per hour, ignoring all other needs, whether hunger, thirst, a nearby potential mate, or, for females, their infants' needs. This, of course, is the kind of thing we see in human heroin and other addictions.

In addictions, we struggle to assess whether something is good for us or not. Your average animal, whether a rat or human, when given food it likes alongside something that makes it sick, will reject such double-edged offers. This is not so in addicted rats or humans, who will go for the reward, whatever. Even very hungry rats will not cross a path that gives a painful shock in order to get the food they want, but addicted rats will endure surprising amounts of pain to get the drug. We see something similar in human drug users, who will, for example, steal from or betray loved ones to get their fix.

Our evolutionary history has not prepared us for contemporary addictions and temptations, such as screen-based games or new drugs. If I am hunting for food and I know my prey or reward is near, I will have a dopamine spike in physiological systems that enhance effort. Something healthy is being sparked here and will keep me on track to reach my goal. This is why the neuroscientist Andrew Huberman has called the dopaminergic system a kind of courage circuitry.[57] This is very different from the way novel contemporary drugs or even social media stimulate a craving and reaching for whatever reward is too easily on hand.

Once I get that reward, the seeking system should lower in intensity, and other areas become dominant, such as for satisfaction and feeling good. In addictions, these other sources of satisfaction – such as the high-status buzz from doing well on a hunt, or the oxytocin rush of loving feelings from enjoying close friends or having intimate sex – are often missing. Only parts of a healthy system are firing, or, to extend the electrical metaphor, all the current is going to one place only, mis-sparking and short-circuiting other needed experiences. Once again, our job with people like Shura is to reset by developing safeness, and then reboot to enable a healthier sparking.

CHAPTER 10

ADDICTION AND POST-COVID MALAISE

Fear, disconnection, and the pandemic

If we had to create perfect conditions for emotional shut-down, for fear, anxiety, and distrust – and, indeed, for addictive traits to flourish – we could hardly do better than Covid-19, its lockdowns, and the nervousness and apprehension it has generated. As we have seen, threat leads to a turning inwards, away from connection, from trust and hope. At the time of writing, what currently seems normal would have been deemed unthinkable a little while back. People have been wary of others on the street, fear-induced distrust written on faces, aversion and even disgust communicated in bodily gestures, and friendliness often greeted with suspicion. The world is not experienced as a safe or friendly one, and other people, even our nearest and dearest, are often viewed as dangerous.

The fear of contamination is closely linked to social aversion and disgust, feelings in which brain areas such as the insula are very active. This might have sensible evolutionary roots – a kind of behavioural immune system that avoids the risk of exposure to pathogens, but one with unfortunate side-effects. It does not feel good to be the object of disgust, to be viewed as 'untouchable', as a potential pathogen. Ostracism and emotional rejection can literally be painful, firing up circuitry in the brain similar to that for physical pain. During the pandemic, my clients who seemed least affected were those with obsessional traits, who were already zealous about hygiene, already somewhat closed down, distrustful, and anxious.

The world was by no means perfect pre-pandemic, but then people hugged and kissed each other readily, shook hands with strangers, didn't think twice about handling objects after others had touched them, or about breathing the same air as others on public transport or in indoor spaces. Touch itself is so important: it has powerful neurochemical effects, including oxytocin release, which is linked to loving warm feelings and, of course, to trust as well as generosity. It is also good for our health. Solitude, isolation, the lack of touch are all linked to physical and emotional ill-health and are proven risks to health and morbidity.[58]

Many colleagues have been inundated with referrals for psychotherapy since the pandemic, while many current clients report increasing levels of anxiety and depression. Studies suggests that there has been a huge increase in depression, anxiety, as well as suicidality, and, of course, in substance misuse. This is classic desparking. Of course, it is feeling safe, loved, and connected that gives rise to hope and spark, and any one of us can, and probably has, felt desparked by the effects of isolation, lockdowns, and the climate of fear. We all have some addictive tendencies, and many of us have seen those impulses and urges increase during this time. Obesity has increased dramatically, as have alcohol use and screen-based activities such as gaming, unfocused internet browsing, and social media activities. I can own that I am more knowledgeable about football gossip than ever before!

Recovering from deadness and addiction: Chuck

There is much in the modern world that increases the tendency to act in addictive ways. Modern recreational drugs fire up unthinkable surges of dopamine, unlike anything humans have evolved to expect, and have powerful addictive potential, often giving rise to terrible 'lows' after use. Much social media and tech powerfully keep us coming back for more 'Likes' or novelty. Large spikes in dopamine levels are seen in what are called 'variable rewards',[59] which describes the uncertainty about what a reward will be and when it will come. We see this, for example, when playing slot machines, and variable-reward algorithms are powerfully designed into addictive activities such as pornography, gaming, and social media.

Twenty-year-old Chuck was an only child whose early life was difficult. His mother had died when he was a toddler, after a long illness. He was raised by his father, who was strict, had obsessional traits, and struggled with empathy. As Covid hit and his university closed, he returned to live at home with his father, with whom he had an uneasy relationship.

He upped his pre-Covid defences, spending a lot of time alone playing computer games or on social media. The good social connections and loving relationships needed to maintain spark were now in scant supply. When younger, he had been unconfident and something of a loner, and he now reverted to type. Previously, he had been doing ok at university, making friends and acquaintances in his halls of residence, in lectures and clubs he had joined, rubbing along with others, and developing a reasonably full life.

In adolescence, he had briefly found his way into a 'goth' peer group and experimented with drugs, including new manufactured ones that trigger massive surges of dopamine. He described being taken out of a colourless world by these experiments. He lost his peer group when his father moved home, and his sense of isolation redoubled. He struggled with addictive cravings, although he did manage to kick the drugs in time. Before university he had spent more time than was healthy on screens, but at college, with more social contact, he had managed to keep this under control.

When Covid arrived, he had to return to his father's house, in another part of the country. The isolation came back, along with the sense of flatness and hopelessness. I had been seeing him in person in his university town, and during lockdown we managed to maintain video sessions, but he seemed to have turned away from hope, felt low, and had little motivation.

Chuck was at risk anyway, as he had missed out on an early life that offered needed rewards, such as basking in adoration, or empathic reciprocity. His father was anxious and rigid when he was young, and Chuck was not a child whose smile would have been met with beaming, doting responses. In fact, dopamine levels of babies born to depressed mothers are lower than average after only a few months,[60] which is not surprising, as rewarding experiences are lacking. Similarly, oxytocin, central to loving feelings, trust, and generosity, is lower in children who experience neglect.

His diffidence and closed-upness probably stemmed from his early experiences, and he was a young man unable to find and embrace hope and a lifegiver. The fact that Chuck resorted to gaming, pornography, and social media was easy to understand.

Setting people up for addictions

Rat studies give us a clue about this process. Rats placed alone in a cage with two bottles, one with heroin and the other with water, continually went back for the heroin and became addicted. Such studies were used to suggest that it was the availability of the drugs that was the problem. Yet, some years later, this was re-thought, when rats were placed in enriched cages, with lots of other rats, including peers and sexual partners, and much interesting play equipment.[61] These rats had the same choice between bottles of heroin and water, but this time the heroin went almost untouched. They had full, rich lives, not the deadened unsparked ones of the solitary rats, and did not need the compensation of heroin to help them feel better. Chuck's life, and many of our lives might, during lockdowns, resemble rats forced from a rich and very social cage into a bare, isolated one.

Something similar was seen after the Vietnam War. During the war, most US soldiers used heroin to help manage the feelings that were stirred up. After the war, though, only a minority of soldiers continued to use heroin, and these were likely to have experienced childhood trauma or have less of a sense of belonging.[62] Those soldiers who came back to rich lives, good relationships, and careers and were embedded in communities, rarely returned to heroin. While we might bemoan the addictive pulls of gaming, pornography, and many drugs, it is a world lacking genuine reward and satisfaction – and, of course, a world of too much stress and trauma – which leads to a predisposition for addictions.

Thus, when feeling low and flat, it makes sense to reach for that which might provide escape from this – whether nicotine, alcohol, recreational drugs, or gaming. Using recreational drugs stimulates the brain's reward circuitry and can make someone feel temporarily more 'alive'. Anhedonia, that lack of enjoyment of life, goes with low dopamine levels. In fact, taking drugs that lower dopamine, such as some antipsychotic medications, leads to anhedonia. When an addictive drug's effects wear off, we see an anhedonic slump, which is exactly when good support is essential, to avoid relapse and a return of cravings.

To make things worse, dopamine, when stimulated by drugs such as cocaine, can even regulate which genes get turned on or off, by transforming malleable stem cells into dopamine neurons, something called *dopaminylation*.[63] This leads to many more dopamine genes being expressed, rewiring the brain's reward circuitry and predisposing people to more addiction. Recovery is no simple task!

Recovery

Before Covid, Chuck was becoming more trusting of therapy, if not quite believing that I had his interests at heart, or that he could be interesting to me. After all, that was not his early experience of adult men. During pandemic video sessions I felt that he withdrew again, and it was a big relief when we could meet face to face again. I had missed being able to use body-informed ways of sensing and whispering to his nervous system, to read his cues and help him read them too, such as the subtle signs of when he was getting anxious or upset – quickening breathing, a slouching posture, a tensing of muscles.

Lockdown had left him more at risk, isolated, lacking confidence, his main human contact becoming his increasingly anxious father who was struggling with his own mental health. We worked hard to think about help he could access. On his return, he joined an online university-funded support group, grateful to meet others and share difficult lockdown experiences, feeling huge relief in knowing he was not alone in his dark feelings. Once again, good emotional connection, even on screen, is rewarding and safening.

Via the support group, Chuck found his way to becoming a helper of others, supporting a local foodbank, and delivering needed supplies, a big shift as he had previously barely been able to see outside his own needs or his father's. As he described his new activities, he had a spark in his eyes, clearly feeling pride and a new sense of purpose. He was also becoming more self-compassionate. This led him to confide in another worker at the foodbank about his addictive tendencies, especially gaming. He joined yet another support group – this time, significantly, a twelve-step programme for those addicted to gaming. Not only did he manage to give up his habit, but he also became more interested in the mechanisms of addiction. Indeed, he became something of an expert and even switched one of his university options to psychology, with the aim of doing postgraduate training.

Chuck had developed some hope. As Huberman suggests, the dopaminergic system is not just involved in drugs and addiction but pushes us on when we are challenged, giving us the resilience to persevere. With his newfound confidence, he now dared to hope that he could have a relationship, and he started online dating. Safening and rebooting had come from therapy, his support group, and deepening friendships, and he had also found passion and spark in his charitable work. I was at first worried that the dating was via the internet, his constant scrolling seeming rather like his gaming addiction. I also worried about him becoming addicted to brief sexual encounters, as he engaged in what seemed like a frenzy of delayed adolescent experimentation. In time, though, he found himself in love with someone with whom he entered a long-term relationship. Like the rats in the enriched cages as opposed to the solitary, isolated ones, for the time being at least he no longer needed the old addictions as he had a rewarding life, sparked by interest, self-belief, love, and hope.

Dopamine – the courage hormone: Peter

Andrew Huberman has helpfully pointed out how the dopaminergic system, when not overstimulated and out of balance, allows us to pursue goals, keep on task, not give up, and enjoy a challenge. This system can turn off when hope, confidence, enthusiasm, and our lifegiver desert us, which can lead to this system being hijacked by easy access to contemporary temptations, such as screens or drugs.

The kind of reward system we want is, I believe, one that can fuel us when we feel like giving up, keeping us motivated when there is a long road ahead. This confirms what the neuroscientist Richie Davidson found in secure, outgoing toddlers and adults.[64] The ones who moved towards experiences with an open, positive state of mind, with a sparking lifegiver, showed higher activation in left prefrontal brain areas associated with positive feelings. Mindfulness gives rise to a similar leftward shift in prefrontal brain activation, linked to hope and an approach, rather than avoidance, mindset.

I saw this with Peter, a fragile 4-year-old who easily retreated into despondency. After his birth, his father became ill, and his mother was depressed, anxious, and somewhat emotionally labile. Peter lacked life, zest, and spark and was a sad, unconfident boy. He often attempted something, failed, and collapsed into a sad heap. He was too young to have proper addictions, but he did retreat into repetitive rituals to calm or numb himself, like hand wringing, rocking, or sensorily stimulating activities like pouring sand from one container into another.

In one session, we were building a toy house with wooden blocks, and it was about to fall. I tensed, preparing myself for pieces to scatter everywhere, which in the past would have led to Peter collapsing in forlorn despair. As the pieces hit the floor, I gathered myself and managed to shout 'Crash' loudly, trying to express the force, impact, and shock, but also convey that this was manageable, even exciting. In effect, I was turning towards experience not away.

Peter had been about to give up, his top lip quivering, when I retrieved a few bricks and said, 'We can make it again, look', trying to model hope and the possibility of recovery. I replaced some pieces, and he looked at me, trying to take in that disaster could be recovered from. When we had repaired it, he wanted to start building the house all over again, now with an almost enjoyable anticipation of the previously dreaded crash. Hope was restored, he did not give up, and in forthcoming weeks this scene was re-enacted over and over. It was as though he was practising hope, resilience, and effort, as if his lifegiver was being turned on. I felt like a proud dad!

Like any of us, Peter needed someone else to hold on to hope for him, something his mother could not at this time do. He developed confidence from new games, such as leaping between pieces of furniture. In my early days of being a therapist, I might have felt I should empathise with his obvious fear and anxiety, but now I knew he needed me to show trust in his potency, not just stay with his fear. When he nearly gave up and I said 'Perhaps Peter can do it . . .', he could persevere. His subsequent attempts were followed by my triumphant 'Yes, you did it!' The resulting smile was his reward system lighting up, showing pleasure and excitement. I had helped him to have hopeful positive feeling-states that luckier children take for granted. Soon Peter was doing this unaided, indeed becoming so lively that his parents worried that he was becoming 'naughty'!

Peter needed help to develop a sense of optimism and agency. Obviously, there can be dangers in overestimating one's ability, but children like Peter run the opposite risk, of too easily giving up and becoming hopeless. Initially the animals he played with were hyper-careful of each other, and, for example, if one was sad or hurt, he immediately got another animal to soothe it. With some kids, such empathy would be a win, but Peter needed to know that his strength, power, and agency could be tolerated, and that a bit of hurt could be recovered from. I learnt to emphasise the robustness of the animals, how they could fight, climb, shout, make demands, be boisterous and lively, and not be cowed by the sadness or anger of the other. Soon we were both being lively and challenging, with the toy animals but also in physical games, like good old-fashioned rough-and-tumble, roughhousing play.

While few parents, in fact, want more boisterous kids, some children, like Peter, can be too fragile and need help to become robust and sparky. Luckily his father was recovering, and the parents were also getting help and were now more able to encourage Peter's strength and liveliness. By the end, he had zest, agency, strength, and the capacity to pursue rewards with energy. He could now hold his own in the playground, had more friends, was invited on playdates, and was becoming popular. In effect, he was developing a strong back and an enjoyably wild heart.

Such traits – courage, hope, determination, even aggression – help drive us forward, as in the determination of a hunter, or when daring to fight rather than flee under pressure. It is a good feeling, linked to potency and efficacy, to what is often called the 'growth mindset'. Unlike the buzzy hits experienced with addictive drugs or indeed gaming or pornography, healthy dopamine hits come from the buzz of multiple small rewards, from pleasure in mastery, from moving forward steadily when we believe this will in time lead to success.

Chuck and Peter, like all of us, needed to activate systems that drive us towards goals, towards and not away from the good things that life has to offer, to have strength (a strong back), open heartedness (soft front), and energy, zest, and determination (a wild heart).

Huberman quotes research by a psychiatrist, Robert Heath, in the 1960s. Heath used electrodes to stimulate brain regions that elicit a wide range of emotional responses, such as sexual feelings, forms of euphoria, as occurs with drugs, and various other feeling states.[65] Perhaps surprisingly, the stimulation the participants liked most and wanted more of was of the brain area central to courage, taking risks, and facing threats. It seems that we want some manageable frustration and the capacity to push through it. In other words, resilience, and the ability to thrive under pressure, are crucial capacities.

Initially Chuck and Peter were given up, turned away; they

had little spark and were damped down. Many of us have felt like that during pandemic lockdowns and struggled to come back into the world with open hearts and strong backs. It can be tempting to take the easiest path out of dulled-down states, using addictive activities such as perseverative rituals, screens, social media, pornography, or drugs. Ultimately these are never satisfying. Thankfully Chuck, and indeed Peter and Shura, were all able to reset and reboot sufficiently to allow their lifegiver to be sparked into action, prepping them for the possibility of being active players in the risky but exciting hurly-burly of life.

CHAPTER 11

MIND OVER MOTHER

Mind-parents

I have met many people over the years who are intellectually bright, minds as sharp as razors, have succeeded academically, are quick-thinking, but have something deadened and hard to reach in them. Such people are 'in their heads' and out of touch with their feelings. Donald Winnicott, in a classic paper from the 1950s,[66] described how some people never quite learn to properly live in their own bodies and, instead, retreat into their minds. In his language, their psyches never got to reside in their somas. By this he meant that when we feel safe and held – for Winnicott, this is by our mothers – we can let go into what he calls 'going-on-being',[67] an experience of deep ease and relaxation, which is very different from the edgy, over-alert 'doing' and active thinking so common in today's world.

Some, like Jana and Jed, whom I introduce shortly, lacked the experience of safeness and calm that allows the possibility of relaxed going-on-being. Infants feeling stressed or unsafe, though, must resort to alternative ways of holding themselves together, including the use of a precocious and overactive mind.

Winnicott knew very well about the difference between feeling alive as opposed to being depressed or damped down. He was quoted as saying, as an older man, 'May I be alive when

I die.' Most of the 'mind-dependent' people I have met have lacked such a deep sense of ease and often are cut-off from emotional and bodily feelings. To avoid a hidden deadness, it is possible to use one's mind to enliven oneself, but the spark gained does not run very deep. The parallels with addictive processes are clear. Deadness is defended against, often fiercely – in this case with mental activity, which can in itself be addictive.

Dazzling false sparks: Jana

Jana was bright, astute, lively, yet there was something hard to reach and pin down in her, something mercurial. Her mother was depressed, withdrawn, with alcoholic tendencies; she was brought to life temporarily by the arts, theatre, music, the opera, but sadly she did not find her children life-enhancing. Jana was raised largely by nannies and was sent to boarding school before adolescence. Her father was a journalist and writer, and the house was filled with books. As Jana recounted, as well as the nannies, she was in part brought up by books, as well as by her fierce independence. Jana, probably like her mother, could seem interesting, lively, and did not obviously show the kind of damped feelings I have described elsewhere in this book. However, inside there was a deadness. Interestingly, I often felt hollow and somewhat depressed when with her and afterwards, something I have experienced with others with similar presentations.

In the absence of a holding empathic parent, Jana had to look after herself, relying on her mind, which became the bootstrap that she pulled herself up by to get through life. We can think of this as a 'mind-parent' – what others have described as a mind-object,[68] in which the mind becomes an alternative to an actual parent to rely on. The cost for Jana was not really trusting others, nor feeling safe, easeful, or fully alive. While Jana did not obviously fit the desparked category, as she could appear quite sparky, her energy and charge were masking a form of internal numbness, one that was hard to reach.

Such a fierce attachment to minds and mental agility can feel lifesaving, but it is a poor alternative to living from an inner wellspring of ease and trust. The spark of such people is defensive and not fuelled by a genuine lifegiver. They can seem likeable, yet often others feel kept away by them. At a deep level, they do not believe that anyone can be reliably there for them, and they rely on their precocious minds in the absence of safe attachment figures. In the end, this tactic often fails. In fact, it did for me: I, too, overused my mind, never completely trusting others, until this no longer worked – until, as often happens, unpalatable emotional realities had to be faced.

Jana came to see me in her late twenties after having something of a breakdown when another relationship failed and she hit a wall, a depressive collapse, her 'false-self' sparkiness sputtering and grinding to a halt. By the time she came to therapy she was in a state of near torpor, in tears at the slightest thing, despite being someone who could not remember ever having cried before. She was experiencing a walking-in-treacle heaviness, occasionally temporarily escaped from by her old sharp wit and impressive mental agility. But this soon petered out, returning her to the depression she was trying to flee.

Mind-dependent personalities are built on shallow foundations, more like shifting sands. Their minds have to keep moving to stay buoyant, in a manic over-energetic way. Jana had always felt like she was walking on thin ice. Donald Winnicott, to whom I owe most of my understanding about such states of mind, once suggested that the breakdown that is feared is, in fact, one that happened long ago.[69] In Jana's case this would have been in her infancy, when she would have suffered dreadful aloneness and a lack of loving holding.

We should have deep respect for the amazing rear-guard action put up by such precocious minds. Jana's defensive use of her mind was clutched onto tightly as to a life-raft, as if only her mind could keep her head above water, painful vulnerability warded off with a false mind-driven independence.

As Jana's defences broke down, we unearthed depths of despair and loneliness. She needed to collapse for a bit, to let go into what was recently called 'wintering' by the writer Katherine May,[70] or what the Jungian-influenced poet Robert Bly called 'time in the basement kitchen'.[71] This is a kind of turning off, hibernating, and resetting, a time for being still, retreating, crying many tears, staring into space, and, most importantly of all for Jana, allowing herself to be looked after by others for the first time in her life.

This included one special friend who let her just hang around her house for days on end, another who came around with food and clean clothes, and of course a lot of time lying on the therapy couch. Here she was able to slowly let herself experience depths of despair and sadness that she was surprised to find, with multiple tissue boxes emptied with relief as she allowed long-buried grief to be felt. In time, the tears ran their course, and she became less fearful of such feelings.

I had a similar experience myself in my late twenties when I had something of a breakdown as my world unravelled, after a longed-for relationship had led to rejection, my work lost its appeal, and my paper-thin late-adolescent confidence disappeared. I, too, needed my few good friends to retreat to and shed tears with, stare a lot, and in effect have a depression that was the breakdown I, too, had long been fleeing from. I had a lot of therapy then too. Slowly I recovered, and my psyche grew back stronger, less defensive, less brittle, with more capacity to bear pain and vulnerability. If I were a tree, I would say that until then I had had very shallow roots and was always at risk of being blown over. Now, though, there was some solidity, enough to allow me to embark on a new career as a psychotherapist, believing that I had sufficient emotional capacity, no longer feeling a fraud, leaving behind the impostor syndrome that I had felt for much of my life. Jana's, and my, process followed the pattern described already in relation to the cell danger response, needing sufficient safeness for a quieting, resetting, rebooting, and, only then, genuine sparking.

Jana in therapy developed a more capacious container, one that could manage grief and despair. Instead of her previous incessant activity, skating on thin ice with her agile mind, she could allow herself to feel safely held for perhaps the first time in her life. This shift made her a better friend and more relaxing to be around, especially as she could now bear sadness, vulnerability, and upset in others and herself, without fleeing into intellectual defences. In time, she developed a different life. She was no longer the same witty life of the party, but she now had a new depth and ease, was able to be more present and steadier in her burgeoning career, and had deeper friendships and intimacy. I, like her friends and family, felt more met and valued and that I was with a feeling-full easeful human being rather than a brittle livewire.

Skating on thin ice: Jed

Jed, too, had an extraordinarily fine mind, achieved well academically, and had many intellectually stimulating relationships. He relied on his mind relentlessly, was fiercely proud of it, yet it was not the core of who he felt he was. He often said, 'I wish my mind would give me a break.' As with Jana, often in sessions I sat beguiled by his sparkling thinking, yet I could lose touch with myself as an embodied person, my mind racing but losing awareness from the neck down.

Jed's reliance on his mind had stood him in good stead for most of his 35 years. He had been a star pupil at school, attended elite universities, and excelled in many spheres, such as public speaking and the stage. There was, though, always a sense that he, like Jana, was skating on thin ice. As a toddler, Jed had been adopted into a loving, well-educated family. Already, by then, important priors had been formed, especially the need to be hyper-independent rather than rely on anyone. He liked getting approval from others for achievements, but this only ever lasted until the next test, and he felt that he was always on the edge of failing, of being found out, often feeling an impostor.

It is easy to be dazzled by brilliant minds, such as Jed's and Jana's, and be fooled by their propaganda, as indeed they can be fooled by themselves. As a therapist, I have often felt I was doing really good work, only to realise that I had been 'taken in' by a polished front, by superficially pseudo-perceptive 'therapy-talk'.

In people like Jana and Jed, we see a mind–body split. They rarely really know their own feelings and body sensations, and they struggle to read their own emotions. This awareness of the subtleties of body states and sensations – generally called interoception and what I am calling nervous-system whispering – is vital for being in touch with one's emotions. Western culture, including our academic institutions, and also some psychotherapies, can overly privilege the mind and thinking over non-verbal realms such as body awareness.

Instead of paying attention to Jed's beguiling words, I tried to stay attuned to where the emotional aliveness was, the feeling charge, especially to hints of striated muscle tone. Sometimes a flicker suggested sadness that was being fled from, or a tensing of muscles hinted at an angry feeling, or a furrowed brow suggested anxiety. I often had to brace myself to interrupt his brilliant flow, feeling as if I were rudely puncturing a balloon. However, a calm ensued when I did pay attention to physiological signs of feeling states that he had previously been unaware of. When this happened, my breathing deepened, and his did too, and he was able to stay with more difficult feelings, rather than expend energy fleeing them.

As Jed began to slow and quieten, he did not break down, like Jana, into a full depressive collapse, but he did experience pain, sadness, and a range of feelings that until now had been too painful to bear. As with Jana, I saw a calming, and a stilling, a healthy quietening and resetting. It was in such states that I, for the first time, found myself feeling sadness, at last moved by him, very different to my previous feelings of flatness in his presence.

He was undergoing a process that psychoanalysts have called 'regression' – where people let go enough of defences to bear feelings they have been avoiding, to trust that it is ok to go into dark places. I liken it to that feeling before diving into water from a scary height, or that moment when we stop fighting the inevitable, perhaps when we know the tears must come, despite ourselves. After an allowing of long-pushed-away feelings, there can be a relief and calm, and when this happens in our presence, it can be a first real experience of what Winnicott described as being alone in the presence of the (m)other.[72]

The psychoanalyst Michael Balint described a man who sat in silence for half a session and then began to sob deeply, saying that. for the first time in his life. he had been able to reach himself.[42] Words, Balint suggested, can take us away from really being in touch with ourselves. The British psychotherapist Harry Guntrip[73] describes this as feeling 'a profound sense of belonging and of being at one with his world which is not intellectually "thought out", but is the persisting atmosphere of security in which he exists within himself'.

Guntrip described patients who, when they could lay aside activity and thinking, contacted feelings of pain and despair that, when borne instead of defended against, led to profound relief and relaxation. He, in fact, saw Winnicott for his own psychoanalysis and reported Winnicott saying to him, 'you know about "being active" but not about "just growing, just breathing" and your heart just beating while you sleep, without you having to do anything to make them work'.[74]

For people like Jed and Jana, a successful therapeutic journey means moving away from an over-reliance on mental activity. Their 'mind-parent' precocious mental agility has similarities with what we see in addictions. Buzzy bright minds are exciting, but false dazzling sparking can mask an inner lack of energy. In dropping defences, resetting, and rebooting, it is as if we strip out the old wiring and carefully replace it so that electrical currents can at last run to where they are needed. Then, instead of random energy-consuming sparks always about to burn out, we see a genuine recharging and replenishing, leading to the purr of unhurried, efficient energetic being.

Resetting, safening, quietening, and emotional holding open the possibility of letting go of defensive mental gymnastics. In learned helplessness, as described earlier, often the feelings that people need to access are anger, such as about mistreatment and trauma. While we also see anger in mind-reliant states, the main initial path to healing for those who over-depend on their minds is via stilling, finding safeness, and bearing deep sadness and despair.

There are many similarities here with addictive states described in the previous chapter. Feelings that are hard to bear will understandably be fled from. This makes the excitement of mental agility such an attractive place to escape to. In the case of addiction, the escape is via the addiction of choice, such as drugs, pornography, or food. In mind-parented states, it is an addiction to a sharp, bright mind that keeps people skating, sometimes soaring, on an often dazzling journey, but driven by a similar fear of inner despair. The mind-parent is clung to tenaciously as a way of remaining invulnerable, because being vulnerable has never felt safe, there never being anyone to rely on deeply. Returning to Winnicott, usually the feared breakdown happened long ago but is still being defended against, which is akin to locking the stable door well after a horse has bolted. Jana, Jed, and indeed many of us can benefit from giving up our busy defences, quieting, safening, allowing buried feelings to be felt, and slowly rebooting and recharging.

Urchins in the dungeon

It is interesting, if painful, to think about what might be happening in the hidden psyches of such mind-parented people, who get by through presenting a shiny if false version of themselves, whose fierce independence is an escape from depending on others. What is the version of themselves they keep hidden?

Obviously, every case is different, but surprisingly I have often heard a similar dream or fantasy from clients, one that describes something fundamental about their psyches. Jana told me about a recurring fantasy of a dirty, dishevelled urchin girl who lived hidden in a basement. The little girl was feral, fiercely defensive, and would not let anyone near her. She had never relied on anyone, never trusted in a safely dependent loving relationship. Jed, interestingly, had a similar fantasy, of a boy locked in a garden shed, chained so he could not escape, scared and suspicious of people and the light. I have heard similar stories from others, sometimes involving caves, or isolated woods, but often a wild, unkempt feral child.

I find these fantasies telling. Jana had a hidden core that kept me and others away. This was easy to miss, as she could be so intelligently pleasing to me and others. Yet it was important not to be misled by this. As therapists, professionals, or friends, it is easy to assume that when we offer care, empathy, or love, these will be received gratefully. This is far from the case. The feral urchin part has learnt not to trust, not to hope for loving human contact, and shrinks from such offers. In effect, they turn away from and repudiate the lifegiver inside themselves. On each occasion when I have seen such fantasies arise in my work, it has been at the point when trust was just developing, and the urchin's appearance was a kind of warning, to themselves and others, including me, a screaming 'Don't trust, don't open up, it's not safe.'

I have thought of these fantasies as like the inverse of Oscar Wilde's character, Dorian Gray,[75] who seemed to remain young, brilliant, vibrant, and never to get old, while there was a portrait of him in the attic that was ageing. The urchin, like Dorian Gray's portrait, represents a psychic truth that is being hidden because it seems unpalatable.

I have learnt that this feral urchin part of the self needs sensitive care. A bit like with a traumatised abused dog, one cannot offer loving care too openly. One has to proceed cautiously, and with great respect for the reasons that such a distrustful urchin part develops. It is there to protect the self, to make sure they do not repeat old mistakes by naively trusting and getting hurt. It needs tiptoeing up to, and to know that we understand what a great protective job it has done in the past. We also somehow need to help it to understand that such defences are no longer needed the way they once were.

The metaphor I often use is that of Hiroo Onoda, the Japanese soldier who refused to surrender and was still fighting the Second World War in jungles nearly three decades after the war was over. Similarly, the feral part of the self believes viscerally that danger is still out there, that the world of people and emotional intimacy is as dangerous and risky as ever. With Jana, there was tremendous relief when she knew I could see and respect that feral part of her. After all, it was what took her over at any hint of rejection. With me, she could become like a wild street cat, with claws out. We gave Jana's urchin a name and spent much time getting to know her, what it was like to be in her skin, what her fears were, and, slowly, what might help her lower her guard and begin to trust. Jana was relieved that this part of her was coming to be known and respected by me.

The 'mind-parent' is a kind of false self, a personality built on a quick mind, on a belief that it is not safe to trust, that there is only oneself to rely on. Underneath the dazzling exterior is a self that will do anything to avoid further pain, despair, or anxiety. Yet, digging still further, underneath the sharp-clawed urchin is a very young part of the self that can, with care, be reached out to and contacted. As in Jana's case, it often takes a breakdown of defences for this to happen. I have learnt that even when we see resetting responses such as collapse, regression, and early stages of trust, the urchin still needs to be looked out for, and when it appears, it needs to be understood, respected, and cared for.

We are aiming to build personalities with solid foundations, people who no longer need to skate on thin ice to avoid a perilous emotional abyss, who are able to discern when it is safe to trust, love, and be loved. We want them, and us, to experience a world that feels safe, where there is little need to fear deadness and depression. Then the false sparks can be let go of, the personality slowly lovingly recharged, making it possible to feel more whole, easeful, and trusting, and from there to spark genuinely and healthily.

EPILOGUE

Purring engines, sloths, and easeful,
not fear-induced immobilisation

I am a psychotherapist, but also a father, uncle, cousin, husband, friend, colleague, and child of my parents. Like everyone, I want to live a life that feels authentic, hopeful, and alive, and I want this also for my friends, family, and clients. I know too well how much life can be wasted by numbing and damping-down feelings. I need only think of clients who are addicted to, for example, video gaming or pornography, to see the hours wasted – indeed, I know how often I get caught up in unrewarding acts like flicking between computer windows. Work is one of my addictions, and as I type this on a Sunday morning, I am looking out onto a playing field, with kids running around, adults doing exercise, young people having picnics, families cycling, people with smiles on their faces, and I wonder if I am avoiding living my life by writing at my desk. In truth, I also love writing, and seeing clients: it is another way of getting to know myself more deeply and taking in the rich tapestry of life. But I can certainly be guilty of not finding the courage or hope to live as fully as I could.

It is a cliché, I know, but a question I try to ask myself and answer honestly, if with the usual dollops of self-delusion, is what I will regret on my deathbed. I doubt I will regret not going into the office for an extra day, or not doing another crossword, or flicking through screens for yet more football news, but I am sure I will regret not letting some people know how much I love them or daring to do things I fear, like climbing or jumping from heights or spending more time taking in beautiful sunsets. My desparking tendencies will inevitably give rise to multiple regrets, and my writing this book is aiming partly to enable myself and others to minimise these.

Unlike what so many self-help books would have us believe, resparking is not just about being brave, making a few big leaps, suddenly putting on a more positive mindset like a new coat, or feeling the fear and doing it anyway. That is part of the story, but emotional growth is much more complex than that. Real personality shifts are slow, gradual, and often painful – in fact, inevitably painful, as they entail opening up to what we have numbed against.

We can think of ourselves as like an engine that has been sputtering along, with plenty of misfiring, stalling, and breakdowns, but just about getting us from A to B. We might be prepared to live with the engine as it is, or tinker with it a bit; alternatively, we might want real change, and for this the engine probably needs some stripping down and rebuilding.

There is a risk that I overdo this metaphor (and others in this book!), but I like the engine comparison because, when an engine is working well, it has a kind of purr, a free flow of energy, an ability to speed up and slow down with ease; it is responsive, and, of course, using my main other metaphor, it sparks nicely and does not misfire, splutter unexpectedly, or shut down.

Stephen Porges has over recent decades developed a popular model of the autonomic nervous system,[39] which suggests that when we feel at ease, safe, and relaxed, then a healthy ease-inducing version of our nervous system is firing. This allows a feeling of safeness, coming with deep, relaxed breathing, healthy heart-rate variability, a musculature that is lithe, relaxed but not floppy, and a capacity to appreciate being in the moment, without too much anxiety. This is a healthy form of immobility, linked with genuine wellbeing, coming with deep ease and a sense that life feels safe and good. This is where our digestion is optimal, our breathing deep and slow, and our immune system firing well, and it is the place from which we are able to empathise with and enjoy other people.

This healthy form of immobility is different from the kind of immobility and desparking I describe in this book, which develops from fear, threat, neglect, and defending against overwhelm. In these states we see shutdown, which is basically a response to danger, one so paralysing that instead of being able to fight, or even flee, the response available is to quieten, numb, go into a kind of hibernation. We then see shallow breathing, bodily floppiness, a lack of alertness, poor muscle tone, and a contraction away from feeling, into a deadening survival-based state.

What we often see in neglect, in dissociated shut-down states, and in learned helplessness is a listlessness, a lack of energy and spark, which can be misinterpreted as someone being lazy or sluggish. In early Christian thought, being slothful was considered one of the seven deadly sins, linked with indolence and idleness. We live in a culture that is disdainful of lack of effort, of doing little, of slowness. Personally, I am somewhat in awe of the sloth. Sloths are creatures with a low metabolic rate, who move gently and deliberately, who literally spend a lot of time 'hanging' around and sleep a lot, and their way of life is far from the manic buzz I and so many embrace in our modern world. While I would like to be more slothful and feel a mixture of admiration for and envy of those who are, my own defences and possibly ADHD-like characteristics are such that I would too easily get bored.

Yet we have to hand it to the slothful. Humans, and indeed most animals, live longer if they have a slower metabolism. Those of us old enough to remember the James Dean quote, 'Live fast, die young', know why it rings true. Stress, trauma, and adverse childhood experiences are linked with speeded-up metabolisms, low immune systems, and a range of health issues, from heart disease, strokes, even to cancer and, of course, dying younger. When anxious or under threat, most of us get jumpy, vigilant, our breath quickens, muscles tense, and we move faster. People even move faster in busy cities, but slower around greenery, and our heart rate matches this, as does our relative sense of ease. From an evolutionary perspective, the need to fire up to deal with immediate threat trumps any long-term safeguarding of one's health.

As described, in neglect, dissociation, and learned helplessness we see a numbed-down immobility, whereas in addictive traits and overly bright minds we see a buzzier, jumpy defence against deadness. For the former, the move to health is one of enlivening, sparking, energising, while for the latter, a move to health generally entails a slowing down to face feelings that are being fled from, such as grief and despair. However, in either case we first need a safening and reset, a turning off of danger signals so that a feeling of safeness can provide the conditions for later flourishing.

In truth, my idealisation of the sloth has limits. A good life requires both the capacity to relax and be at ease and the ability to seek out joy, excitement, and pleasure. As much as I envy people who can be slow, who relax easily and do not work too hard, I also have to admire those who can easily move between sparking with energy and relaxing easefully. The system we see misfiring in those with addictive tendencies, the mesolimbic reward circuitry, is also what can make life worth living when it is firing healthily. In what has been called a flow state,[76] we are totally immersed, present, without thoughts or anxiety disrupting that flow. In such states there is a kind of efforting, but not a tense, anxious kind; people are concentrating and trying, not just relaxing, have a purposefulness, an aim, and an easeful immersion in activity and in the moment.

We all need to chill out, to take a break, to just 'be', and boredom is undervalued in our culture, which emphasises speed and effort. Yet we need more than only calmness, relaxation, quietness: if that were our primary state, life would be without excitement or passion. We need help both to feel safe, at ease, and calm, but also to get sparked up into excited, reward-seeking, pleasurable states. Psychological health means flexibly moving between states, shifting from relaxation to reward seeking to loving contact to tensing against threat and back again – all part of a healthy psychological repertoire.

Spotting and igniting sparks, blowing on embers

This book has been about unsparked states. I have described those whose energy is low, who have retreated from what life can offer, who have contracted, numbed, damped themselves – mainly out of fear, sometimes terror, all diminishing the capacity to live fully. I have also described people whose sparking is false, a way of avoiding an inner deadness and despair. We all can and probably do get into any of these states. Each comes with beliefs, priors, messages to self that suggest that it is foolhardy to hope, to express oneself, or dare to live life to the full.

I have suggested how important it is to find nuggets of hope, seeds that can grow into health, from any of these states. Desparking arises from a need to turn away from experiences that are too much to bear, to develop defensive manoeuvres to manage these. This includes the numbing, self-soothing behaviours of neglected orphans, the rituals of those on the autistic spectrum, the out-of-body numbing of the traumatised dissociated person, the use of a bright mind, or addictions, to stave off pain, and the killing-off of hope in learned helplessness. What these all have in common is a turning away from life, a contracting rather than opening – the opposite of the strong back, soft front, and wild heart that is a sign of openness, healthy wellbeing, and an active lifegiver.

The unfortunate irony is that what initially develops as a protective defence later stops people from really participating in life. I have known this all too well in my own life-experience. Too often I have not dared hope for what was possible and remained stuck in old patterns that I believed kept me safe, when in fact the dangers I was keeping myself safe from no longer existed. Even now, I often notice subtle tensing of muscles, a pulling away from human contact, a contracted stance against what life can offer. I, like many described in this book, can too easily turn inwards, numb down, or tighten. This damping-down of experience stops an openness to the joys, excitements, and wonders that life has to offer.

I am not describing pure personality types at all, and, of course, multiple versions of unsparkedness can be present in the same person. For example, the neglected me sucked my tie and self-soothed as a kid; the traumatised me could leave my body at times in dissociated numbing; the me who 'learnt helplessness' could give up, or freeze, and not dare reach for the goodness in front of me; the me who could flee grief has often done so by being manically busy in my mind, or by reverting to an addiction like internet scrolling; and the me who can be a bit autistic can retreat into multiple addictive rituals.

I have described how any of us can be helped to come out of such states. Whatever the form of desparking, the best help is always served up in compassionate, safe human relationships with a curious and empathic other who can enjoy us, bear pain, and despair with us and show that there is more to life than our numbed body/mind/heart believes. Early in life this compassionate other is, hopefully, a parent or caregiver; later it might be another adult, professional, therapist, friend, or mentor. We all need someone to turn to when we are in trouble, something I know in myself and see week-in-week-out with nearly all my clients.

However, with luck, and help, we can all internalise such loving, compassionate care in the form of a part of the self which we can go to when we are in trouble, which we carry inside us. Psychoanalysis talks of developing a 'good internal object', and others such as Paul Gilbert describe inner compassionate figures.[15] I have also used the metaphor of another internal figure, what Neville Symington has called the lifegiver. It is this lifegiver, when inside us, that helps us reach out to hope, joy, and playfulness too, in effect to the good things that life has to offer. This is a potential in all of us, but it can need kindling, sparking, firing up.

Central to this is the importance of being aware of body-states and how a lack of spark shows up in how we are embodied. Colwyn Trevarthen and Jaak Panksepp wrote: 'We are born with a moving body, ready to share its rhythms and melodies of joy or anguish.'[77] Sadly, so many of the unsparked people I describe did not develop such a moving body, which can share joys, anguish, and the rhythmicity of mutual interactions. Nervous-system whispering is needed for a resparking that generates an embodied life-force and energy.

I have learnt over decades that we really can respark specific numbed states of mind, body, and emotion, in both ourselves and others. For example, the neglected part of me has needed to unlearn my old martyrish priors, such as the belief that no one out there is interested in my feelings or enjoys my company. This means taking the risk of uncontracting, of opening up to hope, with a soft front, strong back, and, in time, a wild heart. If we develop capacious-enough containing capacities, we can notice when we contract, can spot the triggers, sensing our nervous system, and stay present to and bear experiences instead of fending these off. Through such nervous-system whispering, we develop the conditions from which our lifegivers can facilitate zest, spark, and courage.

Containment and safeness are necessary but not sufficient conditions to really change patterns. There also needs to be some tension and healthy anxiety to challenge our default states, to move from homeostasis to healthy allostasis. Such challenge can be unsettling, and we can defend against things that might 'disturb our universe'. I have too often resisted the risk of embracing the new and leaving aside safe old patterns. Such defensive processes can help in the moment, but they come at a cost. Opening up is scary, but, as the stories in this book attest, it can be life-enhancing – indeed, life-changing. If we develop a compassionate big-hearted tolerance of that which we might otherwise defend against, and if we dare to embrace our lifegiver, then we unleash the potential for more fulfilled, joyful, and genuinely sparked lives.

This cannot happen unless we dare to feel again, to know our emotions and body states, and unlearn deep-seated autonomic nervous system beliefs that suggest that the world is unsafe. This means being prepared to experience the sometimes agonising tingling of frozen states thawing out.

This can indeed be painful. I remember that when I returned to yoga in my late twenties and I practised alone at home, certain postures, especially those in which I had to open up my chest and heart (soft front), would give rise to a sudden eruption of feeling – in my case, sadness and grief – that I was taken aback by. I suspect I had been contracting against such feelings for much of my life. Allowing such feelings was part of my reset. I found sufficient safeness to reset, reboot, and then slowly allow the feelings and sensations that arise when we move towards and not away from life and dare trust an internal lifegiver. Through such internal work, many people, including those described in this book, start to look more open, with a more outward-facing posture, as if they can look the world in the eye and move towards it.

The more we have experienced trauma and being overwhelmed, the more powerful are the predictions of danger, and the quicker we can despark. Healing from ongoing deep trauma is more challenging than from less serious adverse experiences, but the process is similar. Embracing our wounds is the making of us – it certainly has been for me. When younger, I bought and sold antiques for a living, and I often think of Kintsugi, the Japanese art of repairing pots so that, despite the previous damage, they end up stronger. There is a beauty, too, in the repaired pots, the lines of gold wire signifying the old damage, the resilience and strength from having survived.

We all contract against feeling feelings fully, whether pain, rage, or that scary one, hope, and often the scariest of all, love. Such openness requires courage; it can literally hurt. It definitely comes less naturally to me than the curmudgeonly depressive postures I know all too well. Yet returning to the deathbed analogy, most of us would agree with Tennyson that it is better to have loved and lost than to have not loved, to have opened our hearts, to have felt hope, passion, and genuine wellbeing – in short, to have lived with a strong back, soft front, and wild heart.

Thank you for reading RESPARK by Graham Music.

You can sign up for Graham Music's newsletter and other information, including blogs, publications, and forthcoming events, at https://nurturingnatures.co.uk/sign-up/ or visit his website https://nurturingnatures.co.uk/, and he can be contacted by email gmusic@nurturingnatures.co.uk or twitter, or Linkedin.

It makes more difference to authors than you might think, so please consider leaving a review on any site you use, such as Amazon, Bookbub or Goodreads

Below are Graham Music's other books

Nathanson, A., Music, G. and Sternberg, J. (2021) From Trauma to Harming Others: Therapeutic Work with Delinquent, Violent and Sexually Harmful Children and Young People. Routledge.

Music, G. (2019) Nurturing Children: From Trauma to Growth Using Attachment Theory, Psychoanalysis and Neurobiology. Abingdon, Oxon ; New York, NY: Routledge.

Music, G. (2016) Nurturing Natures: Attachment and Children's Emotional, Social and Brain Development. London: Psychology Press.

Music, G. (2014) The Good Life: Wellbeing and the new Science of Altruism, Selfishness and Immorality. London: Routledge.

Music, G. (2001) Affect and emotion. Cambridge: Icon.

And …keep the embers of curiosity and passion sparking

REFERENCES

1. Gander F, Wagner L, Amann L, Ruch W. What are character strengths good for? A daily diary study on character strengths enactment. *Journal of Positive Psychology*, 2021: 1–11.

2. Pontzer H. *Burn: The Misunderstood Science of Metabolism*. London: Allen Lane, 2021.

3. Naviaux RK. Perspective: Cell danger response biology—The new science that connects environmental health with mitochondria and the rising tide of chronic illness. *Mitochondrion*, 2020, *51*: 40–5.

4. Bick E. The experience of the skin in early object relations. *International Journal of Psycho-Analysis*, 1968, *49*: 484–6.

5. Damasio AR. *The Feeling of What Happens: Body, Emotion and the Making of Consciousness*. London: Heinemann, 1999.

6. Gander M, Buchheim A. Attachment classification, psychophysiology and frontal EEG asymmetry across the lifespan: A review. *Frontiers in Human Neuroscience*, 2015, *9*: 79.

7. Music G. *Nurturing Children: From Trauma to Growth Using Attachment Theory, Psychoanalysis and Neurobiology.* Oxford: Routledge, 2019.

8. Friston K. The free-energy principle: A unified brain theory? *Nature Reviews Neuroscience*, 2010 Feb, *11*(2): 127–38.

9. Symington N. *Narcissism: A New Theory.* London: Karnac Books, 1993.

10. Halifax J. *Standing at the Edge: Finding Freedom Where Fear and Courage Meet.* New York: Flatiron Books, 2018.

11. Busuito A, Quigley KM, Moore GA, Voegtline KM, DiPietro JA. In sync: Physiological correlates of behavioral synchrony in infants and mothers. *Developmental Psychology*, 2019, *55*(5): 1034.

12. Bion WR. *Learning from Experience.* London: Heinemann, 1962.

13. Eliot TS. *The Complete Poems and Plays of TS Eliot.* London: Faber & Faber, 2011.

14. Beebe B, Lachmann FM. *The Origins of Attachment: Infant Research and Adult Treatment.* London: Routledge, 2014.

15. Gilbert P. Explorations into the nature and function of compassion. *Current Opinion in Psychology*, 2019, *28*: 108–14.

16. Parnell L. *Attachment-Focused EMDR: Healing Relational Trauma*. New York: W. W. Norton, 2013.

17. Levine PA. *In an Unspoken Voice: How the Body Releases Trauma and Restores Goodness*. Berkeley, CA: North Atlantic Books, 2010.

18. Book A, Costello K, Camilleri JA. Psychopathy and victim selection: The use of gait as a cue to vulnerability. *Journal of Interpersonal Violence*, 2013, *28*(11): 2368–83.

19. Maier SF, Seligman ME. Learned helplessness: Theory and evidence. *Journal of Experimental Psychology: General*, 1976, *105*(1): 3–46.

20. Fairbairn WRD. *An Object-Relations Theory of the Personality*. New York: Basic Books, 1962.

21. Laing RD. *The Divided Self*. New York: Pantheon Books, 1969.

22. Winnicott DW. The use of an object and relating through identifications. In *Playing and Reality*. New York: Basic Books, 1971.

23. Abbass A. *Reaching Through Resistance: Advanced Psychotherapy Techniques*. Kansas City, MO: Seven Leaves Press, 2015.

24. Davidson RJ. Affective style, psychopathology, and resilience: Brain mechanisms and plasticity. *The American Psychologist*, 2000, *55*(11): 1196–214.

25. Rosenfeld HA. *Impasse and Interpretation: Therapeutic and Anti-Therapeutic Factors in the Psycho-Analytic Treatment of Psychotic, Borderline, and Neurotic Patients.* Oxford: Routledge, 1987.

26. Alvarez A. *The Thinking Heart: Three Levels of Psychoanalytic Therapy with Disturbed Children.* Oxford: Routledge, 2012.

27. Trevarthen C. Intrinsic motives for companionship in understanding: Their origin, development, and significance for infant mental health. *Infant Mental Health Journal*, 2001, *22*(1–2): 95–131.

28. Doretto V, Scivoletto S. Effects of early neglect experience on recognition and processing of facial expressions: A systematic review. *Brain Sciences*, 2018, *8*(1): 10.

29. Fraiberg S. Blind infants and their mothers: An examination of the sign system. In: Lewis M, Rosenblum LA, editors. *The Effect of the Infant on Its Caregiver.* Oxford: Wiley, 1974.

30. Winnicott DW. *Playing and Reality.* New York: Basic Books, 1971.

31. Winnicott DW. Communicating and not communicating leading to a study of certain opposites. In: *The Maturational Processes and the Facilitating Environment.* London: Karnac, 1990.

32. Panksepp J, Biven L. *The Archaeology of Mind: Neuroevolutionary Origins of Human Emotion.* New York: Norton, 2012.

33. Field T, Healy B, Goldstein S, Perry S, Bendell D, Schanberg S, et al. Infants of depressed mothers show "depressed" behavior even with nondepressed adults. *Child Development,* 1988: 1569–79.

34. Bollas C. *The Shadow of the Object: Psychoanalysis of the Unthought Known.* London: Free Association Books, 1987.

35. Henry G. Doubly deprived. *Journal of Child Psychotherapy,* 1974 Oct 1, *3*(4): 15–28.

36. Olsavsky AK, Telzer EH, Shapiro M, Humphreys KL, Flannery J, Goff B, et al. Indiscriminate amygdala response to mothers and strangers after early maternal deprivation. *Biological Psychiatry,* 2013, *74*(11): 853–60.

37. Krause AL, Borchardt V, Li M, van Tol M-J, Demenescu LR, Strauss B, et al. Dismissing attachment characteristics dynamically modulate brain networks subserving social aversion. *Frontiers in Human Neuroscience,* 2016 Mar 9, *10*: online.

38. Alvarez A. *Live Company.* London: Routledge, 1992.

39. Porges SW. *The Polyvagal Theory: Neurophysiological Foundations of Emotions, Attachment, Communication, and Self-Regulation.* New York: Norton, 2011.

40. Cuddy A. *Presence: Bringing Your Boldest Self to Your Biggest Challenges.* London: Hachette, 2015.

41. Elkjær E, Mikkelsen MB, Michalak J, Mennin DS, O'Toole MS. Expansive and contractive postures and movement: A systematic review and meta-analysis of the effect of motor displays on affective and behavioral responses. *Perspectives on Psychological Science,* 2020 Jun 22: online.

42. Balint M. *The Basic Fault: Therapeutic Aspects of Regression.* London: Tavistock, 1968.

43. Kungl MT, Leyh R, Spangler G. Attachment representations and brain asymmetry during the processing of autobiographical emotional memories in late adolescence. *Frontiers in Human Neuroscience,* 2016, *10*: online.

44. Tustin F. *Autistic States in Children.* London: Tavistock, 1992.

45. Griffin JW, Bauer R, Scherf KS. A quantitative meta-analysis of face recognition deficits in autism: 40 years of research. *Psychological Bulletin,* 2020, *147*(3): 268–92.

46. Beckett S. *Waiting for Godot: Tragicomedy in 2 Acts.* New York: Grove Press, 1954.

47. Maté G. *In the Realm of Hungry Ghosts.* Berkeley. CA: North Atlantic Books, 2010.

48. Rutter M. Developmental catch-up, and deficit, following adoption after severe global early privation. *Journal of Child Psychology and Psychiatry and Allied Disciplines*, 1998, *39*(4): 465–76.

49. Nelson CA, Westerlund A, McDermott JM, Zeanah CH, Fox NA. Emotion recognition following early psychosocial deprivation. *Development and Psychopathology*, 2013, *25*(2): 517–25.

50. Herzberg MP, Gunnar MR. Early life stress and brain function: Activity and connectivity associated with processing emotion and reward. *NeuroImage*, 2020, *209*: 116493.

51. Oswald LM, Dunn KE, Seminowicz DA, Storr CL. Early Life stress and risks for opioid misuse: Review of data supporting neurobiological underpinnings. *Journal of Personalized Medicine*, 2021, *11*(4): online.

52. Park AT, Tooley UA, Leonard JA, Boroshok AL, McDermott CL, Tisdall MD, et al. Early childhood stress is associated with blunted development of ventral tegmental area functional connectivity. *Developmental Cognitive Neuroscience*, 2021 Feb 1, *47*: online.

53. Fries ABW, Pollak SD. The role of learning in social development: Illustrations from neglected children. *Developmental Science*, 2017, *20*(2): e12431.

54. Christodoulou G, Majmundar A, Chou C-P, Pentz MA. Anhedonia, screen time, and substance use in

early adolescents: A longitudinal mediation analysis. *Journal of Adolescence*, 2020, *78*: 24–32.

55. Montag C, Markowetz A, Blaszkiewicz K, Andone I, Lachmann B, Sariyska R, et al. Facebook usage on smartphones and gray matter volume of the nucleus accumbens. *Behavioural Brain Research*, 2017 Jun 30, *329*: 221–8.

56. Olds J, Milner P. Positive reinforcement produced by electrical stimulation of septal area and other regions of rat brain. *Journal of Comparative and Physiological Psychology*, 1954, *47*(6): 419–27.

57. Huberman A. Dr. Andrew Huberman on how the brain makes sense of stress, fear, and courage. *Finding Mastery*. 2020. Available from: https://findingmastery.net/andrew-huberman

58. Hajek A, Kretzler B, König H-H. Multimorbidity, Loneliness, and social isolation:A systematic review. *International Journal of Environmental Research and Public Health*, 2020 Jan, *17*(22): online.

59. Sapolsky RM. *Behave: The Biology of Humans at Our Best and Worst.* London: Penguin, 2017.

60. Field T, Diego M, Hernandez-Reif M. Prenatal depression effects on the fetus and newborn: A review. *Infant Behavior and Development*, 2006, *29*(3): 445–55.

61. Hadaway PF, Alexander BK, Coambs RB, Beyerstein B. The effect of housing and gender on preference for

morphine-sucrose solutions in rats. *Psychopharmacology*, 1979, *66*(1): 87–91.

62. Hall W, Weier M. Lee Robins' studies of heroin use among US Vietnam veterans. *Addiction*, 2017, *112*(1): 176–80.

63. Lepack AE, Werner CT, Stewart AF, Fulton SL, Zhong P, Farrelly LA, et al. Dopaminylation of histone H3 in ventral tegmental area regulates cocaine seeking. *Science*, 2020, *368*(6487): 197–201.

64. Davidson RJ. Asymmetric brain function, affective style, and psychopathology: The role of early experience and plasticity. *Development and Psychopathology*, 2008, *6*(4): 741–58.

65. Bishop MP, Elder ST, Heath RG. Intracranial self-stimulation in man. *Science*, 1963, *140*(3565): 394–6.

66. Winnicott DW. Mind and its relation to the psyche-soma. *British Journal of Medical Psychology*, 1954, *27*(4): 201–9.

67. Winnicott DW. Primary maternal preoccupation. In: *Through Paediatrics to Psychoanalysis*. London: Karnac, 1992.

68. Corrigan E, Gordon P-E. *The Mind Object*. London: Karnac, 1995.

69. Winnicott DW. Fear of breakdown. In: *Psychoanalytic Explorations*. London: Karnac, 1989.

70. May K. *Wintering: The Power of Rest and Retreat in Difficult Times.* London: Rider, 2020.

71. Bly R. *Iron John: Men and Masculinity.* Boston, MA: De Capo, 1990.

72. Winnicott DW. The capacity to be alone. *International Journal of Psycho-Analysis*, 1958, *39*: 416–20.

73. Guntrip H. *Schizoid Phenomena, Object Relations and the Self.* London: Karnac, 1995.

74. Hazell J. *H.J.S. Guntrip: A Psychoanalytical Biography.* London: Free Association Books, 1996.

75. Wilde O. *The Picture of Dorian Gray.* London: Legend Press, 2021.

76. Csikszentmihalyi M. *Creativity: Flow and the Psychology of Discovery and Invention.* New York: Harper Perennial, 1996.

77. Trevarthen C, Panksepp J. In tune with feeling: Musical play with emotions of creativity, inspiring neuroaffective development and self-confidence for learning in company. In: Hart S, editor. *Inclusion, Play and Empathy.* London: Jessica Kingsley, 2016, p. 29.

INDEX

depressed, ill, long-term
  effect of: Peter, 119–
  123
rigid and anxious, long-term
  effect of: Chuck, 114–
  119
periaqueductal grey, 22
perseverative rituals, 123
playing dead, 8
Pontzer, Herman, 4
Porges, Stephen, 137
pornography:
  addiction to, 102, 114–116,
    123, 132
  dopamine hit from, 106–
    107
  obsessional use of, 14
post-viral syndromes, 20
'power poses', 84
prediction errors, 20
predictions, 19, 20, 144
prefrontal cortex, 21, 103, 105
priors:
  challenging, 24, 46, 51, 56
  fixed, 67
  and lack of expectations, 67,
    69
  martyrish, 143
  non-conscious expectations
    or predictions, 19–20
protective shell and autism, 87–
  97
psychosomatic symptoms, 46,
  56

quieting, 6, 8, 28, 34, 128, 130,
  132

rage at abuse, value of, 41

rationalisation, as burying of
  feelings, 41
resilience, zest needed for, 3
regression, 130, 135
repetitive rituals, 120
resparking, 25–57
  from deadness after
    emotional deprivation:
    Rosemary, 77–86
  following trauma, flight
    from feeling: Mendy,
    31–37
reward seeking, addictions as,
  102–104
Rosenfeld, Herbert, 61

safening:
  and empathic containment,
    62, 91
  and mourning, 81–82
  and not feeling real: Mendy,
    33, 337
  and reset and reboot stages,
    importance of, 30
  roots of in emotional
    connection, 22, 118
  turning off danger/alarm
    signals, 13, 20, 30
safety, contracting and
  quietening in search of,
  6–7
Seligman, Martin, 39
Sensory Integration Therapy, 87
sensory overload, managing, 89
sexual abuse, shutdown state
  following, 29
Shelley, Mary, *Frankenstein*, 4
shopping, compulsive, addiction
  to, 102